MONIKHER PRESS
Newport Beach, California

COPYRIGHT © 2025 ASHLEY MANSOUR
Published by Monikher Press, a division of Monikher, LLC

ISBNs:
eBook   978-0-9962787-6-8
Paperback   978-0-9962787-7-5
Hardcover   978-0-9962787-8-2
Library of Congress Control Number: 2024925836

First Edition
Book production and publishing setup by Brands Through Books
www.brandsthroughbooks.com

Discover more books by Ashley Mansour at *ashleymansour.com*.

THE AUTHOR'S SUCCESS CODE

9 SECRETS TO WRITE AND PUBLISH A BOOK THAT WILL CHANGE YOUR LIFE

ASHLEY MANSOUR

MONIKHER
PRESS

For Bella,

my greatest success.

TABLE OF CONTENTS

A NOTE TO THE READER

I WROTE THIS BOOK with the desire to help everyone who aspires to write and publish a book do so easily, quickly, and with the utmost ease and joy. Everything I've included here—the stories, lessons, and ideas—is to help you achieve your writing and publishing goals.

In coaching, teaching, and mentoring hundreds of aspiring authors over the years, I have found this one core truth to hold true: everyone has a story to tell, and everyone has at least one great book inside of them. All that is required is the willingness to see it through, a roadmap to follow, and an experienced guide to help you get there. If you have the willingness, allow this book to be your roadmap and me to be your guide.

While we all come from different backgrounds and experiences related to books, I know what we do have in common is a deep desire for more good books and good stories to make their way into the world. If your book aims to help someone or make the world a better place, it is *always* the right time to write it and ensure its successful journey to publication. Any quick glance at the news will tell you that we need more goodness in the world. We need more good books and good authors sharing their messages and stories of hope, change, transformation, and possibility, and we need them *now*. It's my personal mission to leave this world better than I found it and to do that by helping as many excellent authors write and publish books as I can.

Thankfully, I am not alone in my mission. You, dear reader, have chosen to embark on this journey too, with your book. Now is your time, and this moment will be a defining one for you in your authorship journey. The great news is you don't have to embark on this journey alone. I invite you to share the message of this book with fellow aspiring authors, friends, colleagues, and family members who you know have a story to tell or a message to share. Inspire them to also pick up this book and go on the journey with you, to discover *The Author's Success Code* for themselves and apply its lessons to achieving their own goals and dreams. My ask is simple: if you think of someone who needs the message in this book, share it with them and help me spread the word about what I believe in most.

Anyone can and should write the book that has been given to them to write. It is within you to do it, and very soon, you will see how.

BECOME AN AUTHOR ON FIRE

We call those who undertake the authorship journey and write, publish, and launch their books with us "Authors on Fire." Throughout this book, you will read real-life success stories from our students who became Authors on Fire by applying the teachings in *The Author's Success Code* to their own writing journeys.

You can become an Author on Fire too, and reading this book is a great place to start that journey. Read it in partnership with a friend or as part of your writers' group, book club, or professional self-development group. I also invite and encourage you to be a part of our movement by joining our Author Ignite Facebook group so you can share your own experiences and successes in a space where we can celebrate together. You can join us at *www.facebook.com/groups/authorignite*.

When you join our group of thousands of authors and aspiring authors, you will be invited to monthly virtual events, classes, and opportunities to connect with me and my team of book writing and publishing experts throughout the year.

Additionally, as readers of *The Author's Success Code*, you will find free resources at the end of each chapter to complement your experience and help you take the first exciting steps to get your book written, published, and out into the world. Those resources can be found at *writingcoachla.com/thecode* or by scanning the QR code below.

9 Secrets Await You

THE 1ST SECRET:

Develop A Clear and Definite Purpose

THE 2ND SECRET:

Conquer Your Mental Adversaries: Time, Money, and Fear

THE 3RD SECRET:

Shift Your Mindset from Craft to Strategy and the Words Will Flow

THE 4TH SECRET:

Become a Master of Time

THE 5TH SECRET:

Become a Master of Accountability

THE 6TH SECRET:

Become a Master of Process

THE 7TH SECRET:

Become a Master of Money

THE 8TH SECRET:

Become a Master of Impact

THE 9TH SECRET:

Go Further Faster with a Mentor and Expert Guide

INTRODUCTION

WELCOME TO THE CODE

D O YOU REMEMBER the moment you decided to write a book? Were you filled with inspiration and excitement, or perhaps a little fear and hesitation? Did the very thought of writing a book light you up and terrify you at the same time? And have you since started working on a book but not found your way to "the end" yet? Maybe you've been toiling away with words for months or even years, only to discover you are no closer to publishing and no happier with what you have written.

If so, you are not alone.

Every year, thousands upon thousands of people take up the proverbial pen, hopeful that this will be the year they finally finish the harrowing first draft of their book. From professionals, renowned experts, online business owners, speakers, coaches, consultants, and entrepreneurs to homemakers, retirees, and those with side hustles, the fact is over 81 percent of Americans want to write and publish a book, but only 1 percent ever actually do.[1]

Why is this percentage so small, and what stops so many people from accomplishing this seemingly simple feat? What does it take to become a successful author, and why is it that so many smart, ambitious, well-intentioned people find the task of writing a book so daunting, if not impossible? Why is it so difficult to authentically relay your story and your message in the form of a book?

These are the core questions I will unpack in this book. I have dedicated much of my professional life to helping aspiring authors of all backgrounds and walks of life defeat the demons, overcome the hurdles, and obliterate the obstacles that hold them back from becoming the authors they desire to be. I will show you why conventional writing advice like "just sit down and write" is not only insufficient but inevitably leaves so many people frustrated, dejected, and disillusioned about what should be a relatively straightforward process. Ultimately, my mission is to help you embrace your desire for authorship, take inspired and confident action toward your goals, and achieve your greatest potential.

WHO THIS BOOK IS FOR

This book is for aspiring authors (of both fiction and nonfiction) who want to get their books out there into the world and make a far greater impact in their lifetimes. It is for those who are brand new to the process and those who are more seasoned yet aspire to achieve new levels of success. Here's how I define success. To me, success as an author means you are able to increase and expand three important things through your book and your authorship: your audience, your impact, and your income. I will show you the secret strategies for doing so.

If you picked up this book, I know the burning desire for authorship you feel. I know that deep down you aspire for more in life, whether that's personally, professionally, or both. Perhaps you want more financial stability in your business or the greater earning power that comes with enhanced credibility and authority. Or maybe you're looking to grow your business and reach more people so you can have a lasting impact in your field. Perhaps you see others out there with a book and you know your message could reach millions too. Or maybe you have the desire for more freedom and independence in your life and want authorship to be the ticket.

Because you picked up this book, I also know that writing a book means more to you than just any other item to check off on your to-do list. It's a deep desire. A calling. A goal you know you must accomplish in your lifetime. A legacy you feel you must create. Perhaps you have this desired destination of authorship in mind but you're not sure how to get there. My goal is to help you do that by providing the roadmap and being your trusted guide. I want to help you become the best version of yourself, the fully expressed human being you desire to be. And we'll do that by unpacking the journey of becoming an author through one very specific form of creation: the book.

WHO AM I?

For a start, I am an author. Like you, I am also an aspiring author, which means that while I have written and published books, I still aspire to write and publish many more. I'm also the founder of LA Writing Coach and Brands Through Books, which I created to help aspiring authors go from idea to bestseller quickly through our writing and publishing programs. I have built a very successful business on the backs of my books, and along the way, my team and I have taught, coached, and mentored thousands of people with the proprietary methods you're going to read about in this book. I have also been in this industry for over a decade at the time of writing and have had the blessing of working on every type of book you can imagine. But my journey wasn't always smooth sailing.

The methods I teach were originally born out of necessity, as early in my career I searched for answers to help me navigate the world of book writing and publishing and inevitably came up short. I knew that if writing and publishing a book felt so hard and so daunting to me, others must be struggling too.

Once I mastered a few key principles, applied them to my own work, and found success, I turned my attention to helping aspiring authors accomplish their goals. As it became increasingly apparent that I was able to help people gain significant breakthroughs and get results with my methods, I knew I had found a way to use my knowledge and my love of books and writing to serve others, provide value, and make an impact in the world. As I began working with authors, I saw incredible accomplishments occur that were beyond my wildest expectations.

Individuals who had struggled for years, even decades, trying and failing to write their first books joined my Book Accelerator® coaching program and produced high-quality, finished drafts in a matter of weeks.

First-time authors who had been rejected by agents and failed to land a publisher worked with us and soon landed incredible book deals—yes, that's *deals*, as in multiple offers from esteemed publishers.

Experts who desired more impact were suddenly sharing their message and stories in more profound ways through the written word and attracting stage appearances, podcast interviews, TEDx Talks, and other media opportunities like appearing on live TV and radio.

Fellow coaches and business owners were effortlessly landing $100,000–$500,000 in new business directly from their books. Meanwhile, others suddenly found themselves working with Fortune 500 clients off the backs of their book launches.

Not to mention my author students who have become professional speakers. Their books became bestsellers and quickly launched their speaking careers to new heights, increasing their speaking fees tenfold and getting them invited to deliver keynotes to audiences of thousands.

It has been amazing and awe-inspiring to see my author students succeed using the very advice and methods contained in this book, which you now have access to. The most exciting thing is, because they did it, I know with certainty that you can too.

I don't pretend to have all the answers, nor do I proclaim to be a definitive source of advice or expertise on this topic. There are many authors who are far more accomplished than I. But what I do know is what has worked well for me and the hundreds of authors I have personally coached in my courses and programs, and that is this: there is a better, faster, easier way for you to accomplish your goals of writing and publishing a book, and you can have more fun while doing it. The tools and solutions I'm going to share with you have helped my author students write and publish books that have helped them create successful careers and launch or grow lucrative businesses doing what they love—and get paid handsomely in the process. Not only have I experienced the effects of the Author's Success Code for myself in my life, in my business, and in the work I get to do every single day, but my authors have experienced it too. Now it's your turn.

A WORD OF CAUTION

What I'm about to share with you in this book may be a bit controversial and contrary to other writing advice you might have received up until now. My suggestion is for you to read this book with an open mind and, if what I have to share appeals to you, to embrace it and apply it consistently and without the distraction of other advice-givers who will undoubtedly have their own unique approaches. If you implement what I teach you here wholeheartedly and without reservation, you will succeed.

Some individuals who work in the world of books may not agree with some of what I'm about to tell you, however. Why? Because in this book, I am going to present one very powerful core argument that goes against what we've been told about who books are for—specifically, who should write them and who shouldn't.

That core argument is that everyone, no matter their education, skill level, or background, can—and should—write at least one book in their lifetime. My mission is to give you the tools to do it successfully.

This bold claim goes against a long-standing tradition of literary elitism and exclusion in the world of books. This tradition prefers that only a select few write and publish books while the masses look on wondering, watching. Many believe that nonwriters should not dare to attempt this feat and that those who consider themselves professional writers only attempt it with great caution. This view is best expressed by Joseph Epstein's incendiary *The New York Times* op-ed, "Think You Have a Book in You? Think Again." Writing is not for the masses, he claims, and most people shouldn't even bother to write the books they dream of writing. He says, "Why should so many people think they can write a book, especially at a time when so many people who actually do write books turn out not really to have a book in them—or at least not one that many other people can be made to care about?"[2] His message is to ignore your heart, your soul, your passion, and your desire and to give up writing a book if you have started.

His article finishes with a discouraging rallying cry to persuade the average person never to attempt the feat of writing a book in the first place: "Misjudging one's ability to knock out a book can only be a serious and time-consuming mistake. Save the typing, save the trees, save the high tax on your own vanity. Don't write that book, my advice is, don't even think about it. Keep it inside you, where it belongs."[3]

How does that make you feel? Does it discourage you? Does it enrage you? Does it make you feel a pit of sickness in your gut? Does it make you think, *Perhaps he's right. Perhaps I have no business doing this. After all, who am I to write a book?*

If you are thinking these thoughts and feeling these emotions, then you're in the right place and you absolutely need to keep reading. Not only is Epstein wrong, but he's missing the biggest point of all. Before we discuss what that point is and the real reason you should write a book, let's briefly examine where beliefs like Epstein's come from in the first place.

BOOKS: THEN AND NOW

In medieval Europe, you could do two things with today's equivalent of $38,000. You could buy a very nice, spacious house or you could buy a book.[4] Books back then were not for the masses, nor were they mass-produced like they are today. Only the very few wealthy, aristocratic elites and royals who could afford to own books and had the education to read and write could enjoy them.

Books have carried with them throughout history the qualities of their lineage: exclusivity, prestige, reverence, wealth, status, and power. Reading, writing, and owning books was something you did only if you were in the upper class, wealthy, and most likely a white man of a certain status.

Thankfully, today, things have changed significantly, but the origins of the book have left an unfortunate cultural residue and produced many of the misconceptions, fears, and ways of feeling and thinking about books today. More than this, they have directly influenced our perception of ourselves in becoming authors.

To my mind, this is where so much of the fear, self-doubt, and sense of unworthiness comes from. Thoughts like *Who am I to write a book?* or *I wouldn't even know where to start* are not simply modern fixations of the ego on our own worthiness; they are holdovers from a bygone era during which most people were not allowed access to the skills, knowledge, and education to ever deem themselves worthy of authorship in their own right. We doubt ourselves not because of some hidden flaw within but because the historical landscape from which books were born makes us question our worthiness, our permission, and indeed our very right to authorship.

The good news is we live in a golden age of possibility where thanks to our technology and widespread literacy, many more people can create and consume books in a cost-effective way and in a variety of formats. Every single person has the right to authorship and can claim it for themselves, pick up the proverbial pen, and write. We have everything we need—and so much more than our ancestors could have imagined— right at our fingertips.

The staggering thing is, even with all the tools, access, availability, and methods of writing and publishing we have today, the 1 percent elite who become published authors has not materially changed. We have more tools for self-publishing than ever before, and yet the number of people who write and publish a book in their lifetimes is still a tiny 1 percent.

That's because the problem isn't necessarily publishing, although it would be easy to blame it as the cause, since traditional publishing has become increasingly difficult to break into over the years. The real problem for aspiring authors is getting the book written in the first place. That's what the secrets in this very book will help you do.

My goal in sharing these secrets with you is to help make books and authorship more accessible for everyone. As you continue reading, I would like our coaching experience to begin. Get a notebook and pen. Take copious notes as you move through these chapters. Complete the exercises. Be a diligent student and lean into learning the 9 secrets that will help awaken the author within you, desperate to emerge.

The following chapters will show you what you must actually do to create a fantastic book in a relatively short period of time (forty hours or less) and get it out into the world. It will show you not only how to publish but how to understand the monetization and business aspect of authorship. It's taken me over a decade and countless hours of firsthand experience, coaching, and self-study to discover a lot of what I'm going to share with you here. These 9 secrets to success for aspiring authors virtually guarantee you can have a better experience writing, publishing, and profiting from your book.

WHO, NOT WHAT: THE REAL REASON TO WRITE YOUR BOOK

Writing a book isn't just about the final product and the jubilation of accomplishing the end goal of a finished, published book. That's wonderful, of course, but the real reward is discovering *who you become* in the process. Your own personal evolution is the real reason to write a book in your lifetime.

Do you doubt you may change in the process? If so, you're not alone. Many of my author students start out timid, lacking self-confidence in their own writing ability, and scared to share the message they feel called to share. Yet at the same time, they are willing to try, to be coached, to learn something new, and ultimately to grow themselves into the authors they desire to be. In fact, in this book, you'll hear from many of my author students who have not only finished great books but accomplished something much better: they've come face-to-face with their true selves in the process of becoming authors. As Yasmeen Turayhi writes, "writing a book is like a fast lane to exploring all the unexamined parts of yourself: you get to learn about what makes you fearful, how you think about and articulate yourself about a subject, all your neurosis about what is 'good enough,' and how you react to challenges."[5]

The personal evolution you enjoy as someone who has beaten the odds, mastered all the unwilling and uncertain parts of yourself, been consistent, been coachable, and been committed to the task is palpable. The newfound confidence, sense of fulfillment, and unmistakable authority my author students gain ripples beyond them, to their families, children and spouses, colleagues, friends, and networks and communities. We write books for something much greater than the slim stack of paper and ink at the end. We write books to better ourselves in the process and therefore to better others as well. It's a powerful personal evolution and one that everyone should be able to enjoy. The personal evolution of becoming an author is why you're here, isn't it?

Who you become, not merely *what* you create, is the greatest gift the book you write can give you. If you feel there is something untapped inside you, not just a book but a more meaningful way of being, a greater level of achievement, a higher caliber of creation, a better standard you hold yourself to, more confidence, more freedom, more ease, and more respect and validation, writing a book is a surefire way to find it. The book, by its very nature, has a way of taking us to the inner depths of ourselves and igniting the spark within us that is desperate to grow into a voracious internal fire. I've seen this inner spark ignite over and over again over the course of my career with the many aspiring authors I have coached and witnessed their entire lives transform in the process. You'll hear more of their stories as you read on, but for now, my message to you is simple.

You should write a book in your lifetime even though you may believe the odds are not in your favor.

You should do it even though critical, small-minded cynics and naysayers may root for you to fail.

You should do it even though you don't yet fully believe that you can or even know where to start.

Not only should you write that book in your lifetime, but you should not wait for "someday" or "one day" to write it.

You should write it now. Today! Because doing so will change your life.

THE CORE PROBLEM AND SOLUTION

"All right," I hear you say. "I'm going to do it. I will write my book. But where do I start? And how do I succeed at this?" I'm so glad you asked!

This question leads me to the core problem: most people do not have the tools they need to start and finish writing a great book. I'm not talking about their writing ability; I'm talking about two other components that easily get overlooked. The first is mindset. Most first-time authors are poor thinkers about the process of writing a book. It's not that they don't have the capacity to think well; it's that they haven't been taught *how* to think about the task at hand. They hold on to so many limiting beliefs about their ability to put words on paper, often from their school days when their English teacher marked up their paper with red ink and destroyed their budding self-confidence by saying something like, "You're not a very good writer."

Sadly, I hear stories like this every single day, but you don't need to allow what your English teacher told you way back when to influence the rest of your life! We will cover this topic fully in the chapters to come in order to ensure that you have the right mindset going into the process and that you no longer fall victim to phrases like, "writing a good book takes years" or "you need to be a professional writer to write a book." In fact, if you pay attention, you'll notice that my aim is not only to teach you *how* to think about this but to change your mindset forever.

The second thing that gets overlooked is strategy. Strategy is the method we use to get ourselves from A to Z, from the idea for the book to the final word and beyond. It baffles me that so few people consider their writing strategy when they set out to write a book. We have strategies for everything these days—for starting a business, for parenting toddlers and getting them to sleep through the night, for staffing companies, for leading teams, for learning a new skill, for mastering a sport, for losing twenty pounds in thirty days. And yet, when it comes to writing a book, the method to get us from where we are (no book) to the desired result (finished, published book) is often overlooked.

You're in for a treat, because not only will I teach you my proven writing method that helps my author students finish full-length, excellent books in just 90 days and go on to be published, land book deals, bestsellers and more, but I will show you how to apply it to your book as well.

MY PROMISE TO YOU

My promise to you is that you will walk away with the 9 secrets of successful authorship, including the mindsets, strategies, and tools an aspiring author needs to finish writing an amazing book they can be proud of and get it out into the world. Once you have these 9 secrets at your fingertips, there is no limit to what you can create. You will not only be able to beat the odds and become part of the 1 percent who accomplishes the goal of writing and publishing a book, but you will prove everyone who ever doubted or questioned you along the way wrong. Most importantly, you will prove yourself to be right in the process.

Right in your ambitions.

Right in your desires.

Right in honoring the worthy pursuit of writing a book in your lifetime.

This is it. Are you ready?

Welcome to the Code.

BRANDON WELCH

Coaches are essential. Ashley is irreplaceable.

I have a folder on my desktop called "write a book" that I created on January 1st of 2015. Between that date and August of 2019, I had filled it with fourteen start, stop, and quit versions of the manuscript that had been in my heart for many years. I had been a professional writer for many years, so it always seemed like it should be easy enough to write a book, right? Wrong! It turns out that being able to write was actually the biggest thing holding me back. It was a vicious cycle: thousands of words would hit the paper quickly in a few short days. Then, life would sneak up and take me away from the keyboard for a few weeks. Then I'd come back and rip it all apart until frustration and fatigue set in, fading my book into unfinished darkness.

But in October 2019, something divine happened: I ran into the coach I had long needed but didn't know existed. Her name was Ashley Mansour, and she saved me from what would have surely been another start, stop, and quit saga.

I started working with her that December, and by the following March, my book was done. At first, I thought I was hiring Ashley for mere accountability. And while she certainly gave me that, the relationship was a million times more impactful. Ashley broke down the flawed thinking in my writing process. She taught me how to take boring information and turn it into a magnetic story that people would actually want to read. She pulled life experiences out of me that I was previously too afraid to explore. She gave me the courage to share the ugly parts. And most of all, she gave me the gift of a powerful mindset that has helped me conquer challenges in every corner of my life and business.

With her guidance, my book became a bestseller within its first week. I have booked countless engagements with clients, totaling many six-figure revenues for my businesses. I have also earned speaking engagements, launched a podcast, and even scored my first international client all thanks to the work she did with me in just a few months.

Trust me, no matter how great you think you are at writing, you need a coach. But if you want to write a book that you and the rest of the world will actually be proud of, you need Ashley Mansour.

—BRANDON WELCH, bestselling author of *The Maven Marketer*

CHAPTER ONE

BECOMING THE 1 PERCENT

I T'S RARE THAT I MEET A PERSON who doesn't have a book idea and the desire to someday become an author. The desire is one thing, however. The will to succeed? That is quite another.

I first encountered my own deep desire to become an author when I faced a fork in the road after graduate school. My professor had offered me a place to do my PhD at University College London in my chosen subject. If I accepted the offer, the next four years of my life would be regimented, predictable, and well-plotted. I'd never need to worry about my future because, with a PhD from UCL, I could teach, get tenure, and have a career surrounded by books. It seemed like a good, stable, solid future, the kind my parents had always wanted for me.

My heart thumped in my chest as I considered her offer. Outside, the rain battered the windows of her small office, the hustle and bustle of the London streets a click away. I loved everything about the city, the scent of the cold British air, the swoosh of cars passing along narrow lanes, the pretty lights and enchanting old buildings that seemed to hold mysteries around every corner. I could see myself staying there, devoting another chunk of my life to my studies. And that's when I turned and told my professor I couldn't accept the offer of the PhD.

The truth is, I wanted to become an author. The urge to write creatively was so strong that I set about writing a novel, dedicating nights and weekends to writing while I took odd jobs to support myself. As the novel unfolded, I soon doubled down and realized I'd better hurry up. It had been a year and I was no closer to finishing. Days and weeks went by without significant progress. Hours of staring blankly into space hoping an idea for the plot and story would come to me. Hours of having no clue how to get to "the end" felt daunting and overwhelming. Soon it had been two years of writing, and I began to lose faith in myself and my work. The final year was the hardest. I'm a finish-what-you-start kind of gal, and that meant finishing the book even though it had evolved into something long and unwieldy and hardly represented the novel I'd first started writing. Still, I crossed the finish line, eventually completing a full-length draft of over five hundred pages that took me over three years to write.

I sent off the manuscript to a few contacts in the literary world who had offered to take a look at the book when it was done. I waited with bated breath, nervous but somehow quite certain the book would be a hit. As the replies trickled in, it became apparent to me that something very horrible had happened: I had failed, and failed miserably. The rejections came in, each one harsher than the last, letting me know the work was unpublishable and perhaps I should consider another career. *Another career?* I thought in disbelief. Were they joking? I'd spent three years working on *this* career. What a waste! I felt like such a failure.

The realization was devastating, and soon I found myself huddled on the cold floor of my apartment, feeding all five hundred pages into the shredder, watching the last three years of hard work and dedication turn into trash. It was then I realized that succeeding as an author didn't mean writing *any* book or finishing *any* book. It wasn't about your writing ability or your craft. There was so much more going on!

Some months later, in a cruel twist of irony, I was hired to work at my partner's family entertainment startup company after giving an off-the-cuff presentation on something called a story arc. To my surprise, the stakeholders seemed impressed and wanted me on staff. My role grew quickly at this startup, and soon I was responsible for hiring writers, coming up with storylines for the IP, and, to my horror, publishing books. I knew early on that without my own track record, I'd need to hire experts to help me. So I went after the top authors, storytellers, screenwriters, and story producers to guide me. I also sought out the help of a personal book coach to work with me every week to adjust to the demands of my role and my own understanding of the writing and publishing process.

I received a crash course in book writing, publishing, storytelling, and most importantly, authorship. Not long after, our team began churning out book after book like clockwork. It was here I realized successful authorship is so much more than the craft of writing. Yes, that's important, but there was a clear strategy that went into writing and publishing well and consistently. I began paying attention and documenting what worked and how because, deep down, I had a secret: my own dream of authorship lived on.

After two years and two promotions, I decided it was time to get back to my own writing. But this time, I wasn't going to spend three years writing a book only for it to end up in the trash! I needed a plan—a strategy—to ensure this book would be different. So I got to work and applied the things I had learned and documented from my time at the company working with seasoned authors. I wrote every weekend for about eight hours, and some evenings too, when I wasn't falling asleep over my laptop and a slice of cheese pizza.

Fast forward to the day I finished the book a handful of months later, and I was ecstatic! Not only was it finished, but I had grown an audience on social media that already wanted to read the book. Soon after, I landed an offer to be published and, later, an offer to option my book for film and television. I was on cloud nine! When the book came out, it shot up to bestseller status on Amazon and started reaching thousands of readers worldwide. I would get messages from readers in Germany, Mexico, the UK, Australia, New Zealand—all over the world! My dreams of writing and authorship were coming true, and it felt amazing. On top of this, I was getting offers to be interviewed on TV and radio, to be featured in magazines, and even to write for other brands and companies that wanted my help. Not only did getting the book published change my life, but it changed my career and my destiny too. Soon after, I began working on book-to-screen adaptions for film and television. I even got into film production and helped to adapt the Oprah's Book Club novel *Back Roads* for the big screen. The film went on to release at the Tribeca Film Festival and won a few awards. But the biggest, most rewarding win was starting my own business and helping struggling authors accomplish their dreams of writing, publishing, landing book deals, hitting bestseller lists, and more. Not only had I become part of the 1 percent of people who become authors, but I got to help others do the same.

The world of authorship is incredible, alluring, and everything you think it is—and more. But to access it, there's a Success Code, a series of things you must do in order to become the 1 percent.

So where do we start? Becoming the 1 percent starts with addressing our intimidation about books and especially about becoming authors. Perhaps you've had the experience of sitting down to begin writing and found that you felt instantly zapped of inspiration and utterly overwhelmed and daunted by the very idea of what you were about to attempt. If so, you're not alone. One of the number one reasons aspiring authors share with me about their hesitation to write a book is that they feel intimidated by the process. Often, they will reflect on how they were made to feel bad about their reading and writing skills in school, and because of this, they have never felt "at home" around books. Even those with professional backgrounds that lead to a career of reading and writing—lawyers, doctors, copywriters, academics, and researchers—often find that their deep training and expertise can quickly become more of a hindrance rather than a help when it comes to putting pen to paper and writing their own book.

I have found that many people are intimidated by authorship and doubtful of their own writing. They fear writing a book in ways I cannot detail effectively here but will discuss in later chapters. Suffice it to say that many people encounter some level of fear and self-doubt when presented with the challenge of writing a book. And yes, this even applies to professional writers in the literary field with English degrees or writing backgrounds. Take Joseph Epstein, for example, whom I quoted in the introduction. He's written many books in his career and still reflects on the process like this: "to be in the middle of composing a book is almost always to feel oneself in a state of confusion, doubt and mental imprisonment, with an accompanying intense wish that one worked instead at bricklaying."[6] This mental imprisonment or fear—in whatever capacity it shows up—has a funny quality to it. It almost always causes first-time authors to become stuck, to not write. And even if the aspiring author is able to push past the fear enough to actually write, the fear lingers and creates a protracted, arduous, painstaking process.

The fear takes on a myriad of different thought manifestations as well. Perhaps you've experienced it for yourself? These can be thoughts from *I don't know where to start* and *I never did well in school when I was a kid* to my personal favorite: *others out there are more qualified, so who am I to write a book?*

To that, I always respond with a question: who are you not to? Where is the rule book that says you are unqualified or unworthy? And yet, somehow, perfectly capable, intelligent, goal-orientated people deny themselves the opportunity to become authors every single day. When they rule themselves out, they usually quickly attach subtle reasons for doing so. "I don't have time to do that anyway" becomes a big excuse. The other big excuse is something like, "You don't make money from writing books. I heard from so-and-so that it's a waste of time." Then comes the wistful reflection, the one that will let them carefully put their book dreams aside for another decade: "Maybe when I'm retired" or "Maybe when I'm not doing [insert common distraction or task] and I have more time." Or the greatest lie of all: "Maybe someday."

Does any of this sound familiar? If you can relate and have thought these things before, then know this: there isn't a someday. There is only today, only right now. You're reading this book because you know there must be more to this than the limiting thoughts we tell ourselves. You sense that the things you might be thinking about writing and publishing a book cannot possibly be true, because the fact is people continue to write and publish books every single day! In fact, over four million books are written and published every single year![7] Countless new authors pop up each and every day! Books seem to be pouring from the human collective consciousness at an astounding speed. And they are being consumed just as quickly in multiple formats. Yes, as paperbacks and hardbacks, but also as e-books, audiobooks, podcasts, TV episodes, and even films. *They* are all doing it. So the question becomes, why not you too?

The truth is fear and self-doubt are not the only battles the first-time author must wage. When you set your mind to writing a book, you will very quickly notice how many other fears—mainly surrounding time and money—crop up. Assuming you get past the intimidation and fear in the first place (because you will after reading this book!), there are other blockers about investing time, energy, and monetary resources into the process that stop people in their tracks.

We will deal with all three of the Mental Adversaries—time, money, and fear—in chapter 4, but for now, know that if you want to accomplish your goals of writing and publishing a book, you must defeat these Mental Adversaries for yourself. While there are a lot of misconceptions around fear, time, and money that hold people back from attempting to write a book in the first place, these things are not the problem. The problem is most aspiring authors allow these Mental Adversaries to take over and become far more dominant than their commitment, desire, and focus on their ultimate goal of becoming a published author. But when you understand the true power of your book—indeed, the power of your authorship—it becomes very difficult to let these Mental Adversaries stop you.

ACCESS THE CODE: YOUR READER RESOURCES

As you read through this book, you will find exclusive reader resources at the end of every chapter that you can access for free on my website. Visit ***www.writingcoachla.com/thecode*** *to get your exclusive reader resources, my gift to you.*

Author Success Story

REBECCA DITORE

Even though I've always loved to write, actually penning a book was such a difficult idea for me to wrap my head around, not necessarily because of the writing part of it but because the "imposter syndrome" I felt was all too real. Me? Write a book? Who do I think I am? Who would want to hear my story?

It turns out, lots of people!

Ashley Mansour and her coaching and publishing team taught me how to write a great book in no time and coached me through all the mindset hurdles someone going on this journey for the first time can possibly face, and it made a world of difference. I could not believe how easy the TAP Method made the whole process—so easy that I wrote my entire book in just fourteen days.

I've gained so much confidence since writing and publishing my book and have felt less like an "imposter," because the proof is in the result! I wrote my book from start to finish in less than two weeks and published it less than six months later. It instantly became a multicategory bestseller on Amazon, and its success earned me guest appearances on local news shows to talk about the journey within it.

My memoir is not just a platform for sharing my story about losing my husband and creating a place for his wonderful memory to live on forever; it's a way for me to connect with others who have gone through similar experiences. It's a way to spread support and awareness to those who need it most. That's the true magic of writing and publishing a book.

Imposter syndrome? What's that?

—Rebecca DiTore, founder and president of the
Michael L. DiTore Small Moments Foundation and bestselling
author of *I'd Still Choose You*

CHAPTER TWO

THE POWER OF YOUR AUTHORSHIP

T HE VOICE ON THE OTHER END of the phone was shaky and somewhat quiet. "I have a message to share," Phyllis, the woman I was speaking with, told me. "But I'm not sure how to turn it into a book." As I listened, it became apparent that Phyllis, a therapist with over thirty years of experience, had a powerful book inside her. I could see the potential for a book like hers that explored how abusive family dynamics play out on a national scale, and I could see how such a book would make a substantial impact, if only she could write it. Her own fear and intimidation about doing so was clearly holding her back.

"Can you tell me about your goals for the book?" I asked her, attempting to gain deeper insight.

"I want to help people. I want my book to help heal our country and the world."

"How would it feel to create a book that can do that?"

With that, Phyllis began to cry. She felt the power of the book that was within her, and she believed enough in her message to start writing it on her own. But she was unable to get it done and published. What I needed her to see was the inner power of her authorship, which she would have to step into in order to complete it.

We know the power of reading books. You have probably felt this power for yourself. The stats on literacy improving people's lives are well-established. From improving critical thinking skills to increasing empathy, decreasing stress, and making it easier to fall asleep at night, the power of books isn't just a nice maxim, it's scientific fact. Being a reader means you are more likely to live longer—up to two years more than nonreaders, according to Yale researchers.[8] It also means your brain is far more equipped to develop healthy relationships, read social cues, and form meaningful social bonds with others. Not only does reading books make you more empathetic, but it increases your emotional intelligence. You get smarter, and your brain gets bigger and is more activated when you read.[9]

We know this, don't we? So what's the big deal?

Well, there is another side to this. A side less well-known, documented, and established: not only does reading books hold tremendous power, but writing books—that is, becoming an author—does too.

THE POWER OF BECOMING AN AUTHOR

When Phyllis entered Book Accelerator®, our 90-day coaching and mentorship program for aspiring authors, she was nervous and still feeling timid. I could tell her message was bursting to come out in the pages of her book. And come out it did! After a few weeks, Phyllis asked to work with me privately on her book. I rarely accept private students, but I agreed to work with Phyllis because I felt the magnitude of her vision and her deep desire to realize her goals of authorship. We began weekly coaching, pulling out the foundations and argument of her book, honing her message, and focusing on the development of the structure and her authorial voice.

A few weeks later, to her surprise, Phyllis finished writing. "It feels so good to be done," Phyllis told me, her voice strong, her face lit up with newfound self-confidence. It was rewarding to watch her embrace the teachings of the Success Code, and begin to apply them to her book, only to reap the benefits so quickly. We then began working on the publishing process together, and in another few months, the book was edited and in the hands of publishers. I knew Phyllis felt beside herself with joy and excitement to have come so far, but there was still the answer from the publishers we eagerly awaited.

Becoming an author isn't just a nice experience; it has a myriad of extensive benefits. From gaining greater confidence to completing your life's work, codifying your teachings, sharing a powerful message, and telling the story that's in your heart, books allow us to create a legacy that will outlive and outlast us.

The incredible inner power that comes from completing a book is best described as self-confidence. What I've found from working with and supporting hundreds of authors in my coaching programs, courses, and online author's group is that writing and publishing a book makes you substantially more confident. This is not only because it brings out a can-do attitude that is necessary for completion but because the individual must assert themselves through words. For many people, being assertive is a new muscle that requires an increase in confidence and self-esteem to exercise. You must hold yourself in high esteem to write what you want to write. And to write well, you must write from a place of confidence in what you are saying. This is true for both writers of fiction and nonfiction.

Becoming an author also gives you tremendous clarity. You must be clear in what you wish to say, what message or story you would like to share, in order to write clearly and effectively. Writing is simply communicating through words in the clearest way imaginable. It's easy to not be clear, isn't it? To avoid clarity in our lives, in our conversations, in our work, and in our relationships. In fact, I've found that developing the level of clarity required of oneself to write a book is one of the most transformative actions a person can take. To be clear is to remove all the debris, detritus, and other distractions that take you away from who you really are and what you really believe at your core. When you are clear, you are the most certain, the most confident, the most assured version of yourself communicating what you wish to say to the world.

Let's return to the story of Phyllis. After she submitted her manuscript to publishers, we waited and kept in touch frequently. She would message me, urgently checking in to see if we'd heard anything. I told her to be patient and that good things take time, but truthfully, I was a little concerned. Her book had a big, powerful message, and it needed the right person who believed in that message to agree to publish it. We kept the faith and were soon rewarded when Phyllis was offered not one but two publishing contracts! Shortly after, Phyllis was invited on podcasts and even had a documentary filmmaker reach out to her to interview her for his upcoming film. More recently, she was invited to speak on a big national stage to thousands of people. Phyllis was delighted at these new opportunities, but she was not alone in receiving them. Our authors have been featured in magazines and media outlets; asked to do live television and radio interviews, major podcasts, and TEDx Talks; and invited to speak on large stages, all because of their books.

Becoming an author brings more opportunities than you can imagine. Authors are magnetic. They naturally attract readers and opportunities to speak, be interviewed, do readings and in-person signings, participate in their local and national communities, go on live radio and television, and be on someone's podcast or create their own. The most exciting part is they don't have to wait until they are finished with the book to receive these opportunities. Through the process I teach, the TAP Method, which we'll dive into later, my author students actually begin receiving those opportunities from the beginning, while they are still working on their books.

I realize my authors' stories aren't every author's story. Some books come out and simply fade into the ether, with no one aware the book has even launched. Yes, this happens, and it breaks my heart. But I can tell you it doesn't happen to my authors, and for a very good reason: they know the secrets to being a successful author and how to garner these opportunities to truly thrive.

AUDIENCE, IMPACT, AND INCOME: HOW BOOKS HELP YOU THRIVE

Imagine for a moment what it would feel like to know that your book is reaching new readers every single day, to celebrate as new opportunities you only dreamed about begin to materialize, and to realize your book is transforming your life and the lives of others simultaneously. The more lives you touch with your book and your authorship, the greater the change in your outer world. Yes, this is possible, and books have a unique and powerful way in which they help you thrive, if you know the Code to make that happen.

Books help you thrive in three concrete ways: they increase your audience, your impact, and your income. Let's talk about each of the three things in more depth.

AUDIENCE

Your audience is made up of not only readers but people you can connect with, inspire, lead, and reach through your status as an author. That audience will look to you as an authority once your book is out and want to know more about who you are, what you stand for, and what you can offer them. This is why many authors get asked questions about their process and people tend to pick their brains for advice. I discovered this for myself soon after my first book came out. I was on the KTLA Morning News, and during the commercial break, one of the news anchors leaned over and mentioned to me that his wife was writing a book and asked if I could give some advice on getting published. I was flabbergasted. There I was, with my first book recently released, and he was asking me how to do it? I was stunned. I can't recall what I said, but it sure wasn't anything like good advice. In that moment, however, a seed was planted. I realized the news anchor wasn't the only one who wanted and needed advice about writing and publishing. From there, it wasn't long before I began helping other aspiring authors achieve their goals. Keep in mind that I was a fiction author at the time, and yet I still found myself in the fortunate position of being able to help others with what I had learned. I share this so that fiction authors and memoirists don't count themselves out. You don't need to be writing nonfiction and self-help exclusively to find that your work and authorship can help your audience.

The fact is that whatever you write about, you are going to grow your audience as an author, and you will find you have a fanbase of readers who are interested in you, your work, and how you might be able to help them. What you do with that and how you nurture this incredible phenomenon is, of course, part of the impact you can have and the degree to which you are able to thrive.

IMPACT

Impact is the audience relationship realized. It's the ways in which you are able to influence the lives of others and powerfully transform some small aspect of their reality. That can happen in a multitude of different ways, but it begins with your audience. Once you have your audience, you have the option to continue working on connecting with more readers and seizing opportunities that allow you to do so. Coaching, consulting, and teaching were very natural extensions for me, as I quickly discovered the power of sharing knowledge and key learnings with other people was not only fun for me but something I was good at. I consulted in a variety of industries, namely entertainment, working on book-to-screen adaptations, as well as other industries like online learning and education, gaming, and social media, to name a few. My impact there was simple but powerful: I could help aspiring writers achieve their goals and avid readers and fans get the entertainment or education they desired. All of this was fun, interesting, and lucrative. At times, it was more lucrative than others, so let's talk about the money side of things. Let's talk about income.

INCOME

When you not only build and nurture a growing audience but find ways to add value for people, you naturally begin to grow your income as well. My authors know the secret of how this happens, but most authors don't, and while they may grow raving fanbases of readers and develop an impact with a large audience, they miss the final step. They don't make money. This is primarily because they misunderstand how the making money part of the Success Code works, but later on in chapter 16, I will break it down for you. It doesn't have to be mysterious, but unfortunately, what I refer to as book economics is still largely misunderstood. The economic equation, though, is simple. When you succeed at writing and publishing a good book, attract an engaged audience, and deliver an impact to that audience, the natural evolution is for you to also increase your income exponentially.

Like Brandon, who wrote and published his book with me and then leveraged it into multiple six figures of brand-new business for his marketing and advertising firm.

Or Tia, who to date has been able to leverage her book to increase her speaking fee from $1,000 to $15,000!

Or Cindy, who doubled her prices in her coaching business and attracted many new, high-paying clients since her book launched to bestseller status.

Or Nathan, who generated over $45,000 when he'd only just started the writing process!

Or Emily, who was able to turn her side gig into the full-time job she was looking for in the early stages of the writing process—and secure the salary she'd hoped for.

Or Dee, who was able to fill her entire group program before she ever started writing!

How can one make money and leverage a book that hasn't even been written yet? Again, that's exactly what I'm going to show you how to do in this book and what I teach all my authors. These examples are not flukes. They are the norm for authors who learn the secrets I am about to teach you and utilize them.

In the following chapters, we'll take the foundation we've learned here and expand it to cover all 9 of the most powerful secrets about writing and publishing books that you'll ever learn. These are the secrets that I sought when I first started writing, that I wish someone had shared with me early on. The secrets you are about to read have taken me over a decade and countless hours of dedication, study, and hard work to uncover. Please read on with an open mindset of possibility. We'll talk about mindset a lot in this book, because most of the time when we are stuck, it's because our thinking is holding us back in some concrete way. Once we adopt the right mindset, however, we still need to have a step-by-step plan to follow. And this is where I will add even more value by teaching you the proven writing system I created—the TAP Method—that gets results for all my authors and that I still use for my own books to this day. A fun fact about the TAP Method is that I used it to write the first draft of this very book in forty short days, writing for about one hour per day. I'll show you how you can do the same in a later chapter.

What I've found is that if you approach the process of creating your book in the right way, it's absolutely inevitable that it will get done, get published, and have an impact beyond your wildest imagination. So, from this moment forth, remove any doubt, fear, or hesitation from your mind. You can do this! You *will* do this! In fact, you *must* do this. I'm here to guide you through it, but I need you to fully commit yourself to doing two things: 1) finish reading this book and 2) decide to put everything you learn here into practice today.

To commit yourself fully to these two things could be the single greatest shift for you and your future. Take a moment right now and say to yourself out loud, "I commit!" If you said it softly or timidly, say it louder with force and meaning! "I commit!"

Once you are finished, I invite you to access the downloadable Decide and Commit Declaration located in the reader resources section of my website at writingcoachla.com/thecode. I recommend you download and print this out and post a photo of your signed declaration in my author's community to solidify your decision and commitment to yourself, your books, and the future you are creating. The link to find that community is on the aforementioned website.

Next up, let's dive into the 9 secrets of the Author's Success Code. Regardless of where you are in the process, believe me when I say that these 9 secrets can not only help you but truly change your life if you let them.

JOIN THE AUTHOR'S SUCCESS CODE MOVEMENT

I invite you to join our community of aspiring and accomplished authors right now and share your journey, starting with your Decide and Commit Declaration. Visit
www.writingcoachla.com/thecode
to get access to the community and become part of our movement.

Author Success Story

JOANNA MCSPADDEN

I wrote my fiction book in record time using Ashley's TAP Method, and just getting the book done was a huge personal success I've always dreamed of. By the time we started working together, I had already been trying to write this book for years. I had always wanted to get this story out, but I didn't have the right tools to do so. Ashley gave me exactly what I needed to get it done: a reliable process and endless encouragement.

Little by little, word by word, I started to become more than a writer—I was becoming an author with real credibility! I was even accepted into three writing groups that I never would have had the confidence to join before.

But it gets better! After I finished my book and joined Ashley's Publishing Master program to pitch it to publishers, I landed a publishing deal with a New York publisher! The whole thing has felt like an absolute dream that I can't believe I'm really living.

There is nothing quite like holding your own book in your hands, let alone knowing that people are reading it. I've even been a guest on multiple podcasts to talk about my work and my journey, something so validating that I never thought I would do. There is so much more to being an author than just the writing part, and Ashley and her team guided and encouraged me every step of the way. My publisher has already committed to releasing the sequel to my first book, and I'm even going on to collaborate on a short story collection with other fantasy authors I love and admire—a dream come true.

This experience has been more rewarding than I ever imagined it could be. I get to talk about the world and characters I've created with my readers—my readers. I have readers! What a wonderful adventure this has been to say the least, and what a journey of transformation it has been to say more.

—JoAnna McSpadden, bestselling author of the
Lumos Gems Chronicles

Develop a Clear and Definite Purpose

CHAPTER THREE

THE 1ST SECRET

Develop a Clear and Definite Purpose

L ET ME ASK YOU A SIMPLE QUESTION: why do you want to write a book? What is it about the prospect of becoming an author that lights you up inside?

For me, what lights me up about being an author is the endless possibilities it creates, not just for me and my family but for every single reader my book reaches. I love knowing that once a reader picks up my book, they may be forever changed by my words. Think about that for a moment. Your book in the hands of thousands of people, changing lives one at a time. How would that feel? How would it feel to know that while your book is positively impacting others, you are also enjoying the fruits of this phenomenon?

Imagine for a moment the freedom of knowing that simply by doing what you love and sharing your message or story with the world, you can support yourself and your family and live a wonderful lifestyle. Imagine having more freedom in your life to pursue the things that matter, spend time with your loved ones, travel to new places, and enjoy new experiences, all because your book is making an impact in the world. All because you took the time to write it and see it through to publishing.

All of this is possible. Through writing and publishing books, you can do more than simply earn an income. You can create a financially free future, impact lives, and grow yourself in the process simply by doing what you love most.

Creating the audience, impact, and income you desire from your book starts with one thing: your core motivation, your *why*. When I coach authors in my Book Accelerator® and private coaching programs, this is one of the very first pieces of self-discovery they do. They discover their *why*. You've probably heard a lot about the power of *why* from people like Simon Sinek and others. If so, you know that finding your purpose in any endeavor is key to your success. You cannot wish for something to come into existence without really being clear about *why* you desire its existence in the first place. You have to give the Universe, God, the Spirit, the Source—whatever your terminology—a really good reason to bring it forth. It's not enough to simply desire it. You must have meaning behind that desire and be clear as to what it is. You must have what Napoleon Hill famously termed "definiteness of purpose."[10]

A definite purpose is one you can give your whole self to. It's a purpose that is perfectly in tune with your motivation and that creates an energetic response in you of excitement, motivation, and joy. You can see why that would be important, can't you? When you are excited, motivated, and joyful, you are much more likely to act toward your goal, and therefore the goal itself has a far greater likelihood of being accomplished. But you may be wondering how to discover your purpose. How do we discover our *why*? After all, a clear and definite purpose fuels the successful journey of the aspiring author.

Let's unlock this first secret together.

DISCOVER YOUR "WHY"

Your *why* is already within you. You don't have to go and create it or seek it out. When I say discover your *why*, I'm talking about looking inward to find the reason—the real reason—why you desire to become an author in the first place. If you don't believe me that your *why* is already inside of you, let me ask you, where did your initial idea or impulse to write a book come from? Did it come from within you or outside of you?

I'm willing to bet it came from within you. Even if someone else had the idea first and said, "Ever think about writing a book?" or "Wow, you should write a book," I have news for you. That wasn't coming from outside of you. That was your inner author projecting itself onto others before your mind caught up! We'll talk more about this later, but for right now, what I'd like you to tap into is the fact that your inner author has always been there. That is, the idea and impulse to write a book has been within you for a lot longer than you may realize.

When you really think about it, you'll be able to do a deep inward dive and some serious introspection. I encourage you to truly dive deep to uncover what I like to call your deepest *why*. Your deepest *why* is the purpose or meaning lurking far below the surface. Many people begin this process of unearthing their *why* with a surface-level understanding. But all of us are like icebergs. We all have vast, unexplored depths of ourselves that remain hidden to others for the most part, and sometimes even to us. That's why, as you begin to dive below the surface, I invite you to think about what's really beneath the first or second *why* that you come up with. What is your deepest *why*?

Getting clear on this question may take you to places you didn't expect, but having a clear *why* is not only important for your motivation and the way in which you approach your writing; it's also important for clarity. Having clarity in terms of your purpose will not only shape your writing, but it will fuel you in those moments when you find it difficult to show up to write your book, when you're struggling, or when you're encountering fear and self-doubt.

Having a clear purpose is the antidote to a lot of the negative experiences authors face—experiences like writer's block, procrastination, and starting and stopping, starting but then leaving the book half-finished (as I know many aspiring authors have done, sadly). I suspect that millions of people have partially written books sitting on their computers and don't return to them because they never took the time to really dig into their *why* and unpack it. They wrote without clarity of purpose, and then once the initial burst of inspiration faded away, they simply stopped writing.

Don't let this be you! Find your deepest *why*, your clear and definite purpose.

Develop a clear and definite purpose because it will fuel the writing journey of the aspiring author.

That is the first secret.

So now is the time to get clear and answer the following questions for yourself to discover your deepest *why*.

1. Why do you want to write this book?
2. What is your purpose and your core motivation?
3. What about that purpose excites you, motivates you, and inspires you?
4. What brings you joy from this?
5. How does this *why* connect to you and your story?

When I first did this exercise for myself, I discovered I wasn't really clear about my purpose for writing. Looking back, I'm certain that my lack of clarity contributed to the long, meandering three years of writing that became an unpublishable book and feeling like a failure in the process. I know you don't want this outcome for yourself, and that's why you must answer these questions in more detail than will feel comfortable. Many people, for example, have an unexplainable, vague desire to write a book, but they don't take the time to investigate it further and figure out their deepest *why*. Therefore, their motivation for writing and publishing a book stays at the surface level and never develops into something powerful that can carry them through the entire process of writing and publishing a book. This is why many get started, without their deepest *why*, and quickly lose interest or give up.

If you've found yourself here or have never taken the time to discover your deepest *why*, my advice is to take thirty to sixty minutes to sit down and freewrite responses to the questions in this chapter one by one. The longer you spend really investigating this for yourself, the better off you will be when it comes to writing your book. Contrary to what you might think, this exercise is essential! Remember, having a clear and definite purpose isn't only important for the book, it's important for life. A sense of purpose is very strongly associated with mental and physical well-being and increased longevity.[11] This is science. It's factual, not anecdotal. Though the stories of my authors who have done this are very inspiring.

Take my author Brett, who initially wanted to write a novel about his own story and soon realized through this exercise that his purpose was deeply connected to helping other high-performing men recover from overworking and addiction, reconnect to their faith, and become the content, happy, well-balanced men they desire to be.

Or Lynn, who initially wanted to write to share a simple message that women don't need any extra help but instead need to stop being burdened by society's restrictions and demands. She soon found through this exercise, however, that not only did she wish to unburden women, but she also wanted to uplift them through a type of mentoring she'd experienced in her own work as a state senator.

Or Thelma, who initially wanted to write a memoir for her family to know the life of her late husband better but soon discovered a passion for telling stories of growing up in the Philippines to inspire young children to face adversity with courage and never give up on their dreams.

Can you see how powerful these clear and definite purposes are?

Not only does having a clear *why* and purpose motivate and inspire you, but it connects you to what you really care about. When you care about something, you treat it differently, don't you? You show up differently. You invest your time. You are more conscientious. You are more deeply committed to it. And those elements are exactly what you need to form a bond with the book inside of you so that you can bring it out. This is what it means to be an author.

Now for my last question to you: are you a person who desires a book, or are you a person who desires authorship? "What's the difference?" you might ask. Let's dive into what it really means to be an author and how you can tell that you're supposed to be one.

BEING AN AUTHOR

Before we talk about what being an author is, let's talk about what being an author is not. In my work, I've studied this deeply and talked to hundreds of authors over the years, successful and not-so-successful. This may be triggering for some to hear, but this is based on that deep work and the discoveries I have made.

First of all, being an author is not hiring someone else to write your book for you. Hiring a ghostwriter to write the book is not *being* an author because it doesn't get the same results you achieve when you write your book yourself. Yes, it may get your stories and words on the page, but they didn't come from you, even if you spoke them out loud in the interview with your ghostwriter. So let's pin down a further definition.

Whoever does the physical act of putting words on the page and arranging them into the right order, whoever conceptualizes and actually completes the book by the action of writing, is the author. They are the cause; the words are the effect.

If you doubt this, consider the very definition of an author: "one that originates or creates something."[12] The ghostwriter, no matter how good they are or appear to be, holds the title of writer. Ghost. Writer. They are the hand that authors the book, even though your name might be on it. Energetically, they are writing the book, and when this is the case, the person who hires the ghostwriter does not get to experience the same inner transformation the person who writes their own work does. This is unfortunate because there are infinite benefits to doing so, but they only come about when you actually sit down and write your book—author your book—yourself. They do not come when someone else does it for you. It's a bit like using a Segway to "run" a marathon. It defeats the purpose, doesn't it?

The inner transformation for the author happens in the outpouring of their own words onto the page, in the act of creation itself. If someone ghostwrites your book for you, then that transformation happens for *them*, not for you. Even if you feel pride, joy, and excitement in your final product, that doesn't make it your creation. Being an author means owning the process of creation and birthing the book. It means connecting with and reaching readers all over the world. It means standing in the world as an author and giving readers the gift of your book one word, one page at a time. It is an outpouring of *you* through the act of writing, through creating the written word, not through someone else writing for you. And it means making money from your book, that is, leveraging it in the world and making the most of the opportunities that come to you.

The truth is only authors with a strong sense of purpose actually succeed.

Are you an author with a strong sense of purpose? Or are you someone who wants to have a book but not actually author it?

These are important questions you ought to discover the answers to:

1. Who are you writing for?
2. What is the big idea or premise of the book?
3. What is the main outcome for your ideal reader?
4. What type of book are you writing?
5. Why are you writing this book? What is your motivation and intention (your deepest *why*)?

Once you have clear answers to these questions, you can write something called a purpose statement. A purpose statement is for you and not to be shared with readers, agents, or publishers. It is something you can internalize to help you focus on your book and solidify your *why* by putting it into words. It combines all elements of the answers to the questions above—the who, what, and why of your book that is so important to be clear on before going further and attempting to write it.

What happens if you write your book without a purpose statement? What I've found is that authors who write without a purpose statement end up writing the first draft for themselves, not for their readers. Because they are not clear on who the book is for and what the outcome of the book should be, they write to try and discover that outcome through an outpouring of whatever comes to mind that particular day. This is a slow, painstaking process, and one that I don't recommend for first-time authors. It is known as "pantsing"—that is, writing by the seat of your pants, without an outline and without prewriting.

Many first-time authors write this way, and that's perfectly fine—if you don't mind spending a very long time (perhaps years) simply discovering what you want to say. Once you do, you will have a muddled manuscript that reflects that journey. The next question will be whether what you've written has any semblance of quality to it and the ability to be published.

The publishability factor is extremely important because it determines whether or not your book gets out there to readers. Books are, by design, there to be read. And we should write with the intent of someone else (not us) being able to read and gain value from what we've created. Sadly, not all books are publishable, and not all authors care to do the legwork to make them so. I would encourage you to avoid this trap of writing an unpublishable book and to write with purpose, with your deepest *why* at the forefront of your mind.

A final reason to write with a purpose statement is to bolster your own accountability and motivation. This is perhaps the most important aspect, because when you write without a strong sense of purpose, it is easy to drift. Instead, I encourage you to write with clarity so you can forge a strong, consistent writing habit, get your words on the page, and stay accountable to your creation throughout the journey to publishing, marketing, and beyond. One of the primary things first-time authors tell me they need help with is accountability, and you may find this is true for you as well. Later, in chapter 8, I will show you the secret to developing real accountability.

For now, the next step is to write out your purpose statement. Here are a few examples, starting with the purpose statement for this very book.

I am writing a breakout nonfiction book about the 9 secrets of successful authorship in order to help aspiring authors break through the three Mental Adversaries, realize their potential, and finally get their books done, published, and out into the world so that they can increase their audience, impact, and income!

All of my author students create purpose statements. It's one of the first things we do in my 90-day writing program, Book Accelerator®, and it's so amazing to see how it helps people create real, tangible connections with their books like they've never had before. Once they discover their *why*, their reason, they articulate that in a purpose statement. Here are a few of the purpose statements my authors have created over the years:

I am writing a nonfiction memoir about grief and life after loss to offer other grievers the inspiration and hope to know that though their grief may feel unbearable right now, they can and will both heal and find joy again.

I am writing a groundbreaking book about the real cause of chronic pain in order to help millions of people in pain finally learn the true cause of their pain and show them a proven method of reversing it so they can resume living normal and happy lives.

I am writing a nonfiction parenting book that teaches parents how to create a deep, authentic connection with their children and parent differently than their parents. My goal is to help them release their inner authentic HERO so they can ditch the negative self-talk and self-hatred and shift to truly unconditionally love themselves.

Now it's your turn. Take a few moments to write out your own purpose statement. Make sure the words resonate with you and you can truly *feel* your purpose and deepest *why* as you write it. If you get stuck, use some of the examples I shared with you as a starting point. Don't worry about whether it's perfect. You can always revise it later. I know you have a strong purpose inside of you. The key is to crystallize it and put it into words. When you do this for yourself, I know you will develop an even greater, more concrete, and important connection to the book inside of you.

Now that you've got your purpose statement and you are clearer about the importance of your deepest *why*, let's address the three biggest blockers most people encounter in their journey of writing and publishing. I call these the three Mental Adversaries. Sound intimidating? Not to worry, by the time we're finished, you will be well-equipped to defeat them one by one *and* know how to protect yourself should one of them rear its ugly head in the future.

Gather your armor and your sword. It's time to go into battle.

ACCESS THE CODE: POWERFUL PURPOSE STATEMENT

If you'd like more help creating a powerful purpose statement, download my Powerful Purpose Statement Worksheet at **www.writingcoachla.com/thecode.**

JULIE MARRAST

I worked with Ashley Mansour to bring my soul's purpose to life, something I had been struggling over for years. That purpose was to support parents through a transformation of their relationships with their children, themselves, and the world around them.

My writing journey through the TAP Method allowed me to overcome many limiting beliefs and empower myself to be a voice of change. Its steps provided the space I needed to ground myself in my "why" and enter a flow state where I could live and write from a place of love and creativity. The result was that I completed a book in just 90 days, but more than that, finishing it gave me self-confidence and instilled the belief that I am capable of anything I put my mind to. Ashley's methodology supported my journey of discovering more of my authentic self and offered me the ability to truly live in freedom.

I published my book with Ashley and her team at Brands Through Books, and not only did they provide guidance and insight at every step, but they always encouraged me to keep going. Even in times when self-doubt crept back in, they kept reminding me over and over again of my big why, and that my message was too important to delay sharing any longer.

Thanks to their support and expertise, my book became an overnight #1 international bestseller. Having this incredible foundation has allowed me to launch my coaching business and guide others through their own parenting journeys. It has given me the confidence to do a TEDx Talk and arrange more public speaking engagements to further share my message. It has helped me to realize I can truly make a difference in the lives of others.

If you're thinking about writing a book and sharing your story, I understand that you might have doubts. But if that's the case, look no further than Ashley Mansour and her team. They will guide and support you through every step you need to create this incredible piece of you that's waiting to be shared with the world. The process and the experience will change your life in incredible ways.

—JULIE MARRAST, parent self-discovery coach and bestselling author of *Different Than Your Parents*

Conquer Your Mental Adversaries: Time, Money, and Fear

CHAPTER FOUR

The 2nd Secret

Conquer Your Mental Adversaries: Time, Money, and Fear

WRITING A BOOK is as much a mental game as it is a strategic one. Those who have written and published many books may argue it's mostly a mental game. The good news is most first-time authors struggle with the same core blockers. Experiences like worry, fear, self-doubt, procrastination, overwhelm, and writer's block are extremely common enemies of the aspiring author. All writers attempting a book have them at one point or another. Don't let them deter you. Instead, let's look at how to defeat these Mental Adversaries one by one.

The three Mental Adversaries will undoubtedly come up at some point or another in every aspiring author's journey. Whether you think of them as blockers, hurdles, battles to wage, enemies to conquer, or simply troublesome antagonists, the Mental Adversaries are just that—adversarial. They create conflict and tension within us and impede our ability to achieve what we most desire. And that's why they are our enemies if we allow them to persist.

The Mental Adversaries, once they gain a foothold within us, can be quite ruthless. They can be soul-destroying and heartless, caring not for our deepest desires, dreams, and ambitions. They are particularly insidious because, while they destroy our self-confidence and hamper our progress, they may appear on the surface as the most logical thoughts we've ever had. The irony is their mission is to keep us safe, to protect us from the unknown, to keep us living in the status quo and taking no action to change it. They are, and will remain, wholly against the idea of you writing and publishing your book.

As soon as you know this, you can begin to wage the appropriate counterstrike against these destructive Mental Adversaries. You can defeat them one by one. The best way to do that? Divide and conquer. To continue our discussion and arm you with the best tools to do so, let's begin with understanding what the Mental Adversaries are and how they function in terms of your writing and publishing goals.

THE REASONS WE DON'T WRITE

Let's make it abundantly clear: there is never a "good reason" to not write your book. And yet, thousands of people every single day manage to convince themselves they have a good reason not to write their books. This phenomenon occurs because of the Mental Adversaries and their treacherous work against many aspiring authors. Let's look at what they are specifically, how they influence aspiring authors to give up on their goals, and how they create the core reasons we don't write.

The three Mental Adversaries are time, money, and fear. Any hesitation or unwillingness to write, any reason one gives for not writing, can be boiled down to these three adversaries. By far the most common of the three that I hear is this: "I don't know where to start." This in itself is not a good reason; it's a reason based on fear. What lies beneath this statement may be one or more of the following thoughts:

- *I've never done this before.*
- *What if I mess up or get it wrong?*
- *What if I look foolish or stupid?*
- *What if I'm not good enough?*

- *What will others think of me?*
- *I don't know how to do it well or do it right.*
- *I'm scared of attempting something new.*
- *What if I try and I fail?*
- *What if I try and succeed?* (Oddly off-putting for some who feel undeserving.)
- *What if I try and find out I'm no good at it?*
- *It will be too hard, too painful, too frustrating.*
- *I will probably quit anyway, so why bother?*
- *I don't know enough to attempt this; I don't know anything about it.*
- *I'm not a real writer. I don't have any education in this area.*
- *When I've written before, it felt difficult, and I didn't like what I wrote.*
- *I never did well with writing in school.*
- *I don't think I'll be good at this now, so why bother?*
- *People I care about wouldn't understand or support me.*
- *If I try to do this and it doesn't go well, my reputation could be damaged.*

The list could go on and on, ad infinitum. I hope you will see that all of these thoughts are deeply interconnected and all relate back to one thing: fear. What type of fear? Fear of all sorts of things. Fear of failure is a big one. But they also relate to fear of change, fear of the unknown, and fear of how others will react.

We will deal more with fear, our first Mental Adversary, in a moment. For now, know that a lot of what seems like logical concern on the surface is actually fear, your Mental Adversary, waging a successful battle against your own goals and dreams below the surface.

The next Mental Adversary is time. First-time authors, and even many well-established authors, greatly overestimate the time it takes to write a book. When I mention how long writing a book should take you, what comes to mind? Do you think in terms of years? Months? Weeks?

Hours? Most people think of a length of time that is actually far too long for any book project. For example, I recently spoke with an aspiring author who believed the outline and first draft of his book should take him two years. He didn't feel particularly happy about this length of time, but it's what he came up with.

What length of time comes to mind for you when you think of writing a book? Write this number below or in a notebook so that when we tackle the Mental Adversary of time, we can return to it and see first-hand how accurate your estimation was and, therefore, how the Mental Adversary of time was succeeding.

I think it will take _____ to write my book.

Lastly, let's talk about the Mental Adversary of money. This is a tough one because money is far more tangible than time, isn't it? We use money to live, to eat, to house ourselves, to experience life. We need money to exist in the modern world. Money is also elusive, like time. We struggle to know how to attain more of it and what to do to keep it, increase it, and make it feel more plentiful than it is. We work on having more money, just as we work on having more time, and yet there is a concrete difference between the two: money always replenishes, but time never does. In many ways, time and money feel like they are the same finite forces, when in fact they are opposites.

For this reason, time and money are two very powerful adversaries. We always desire more, and yet the answer of how to *get* more frequently evades us. Our deep desire to make them more plentiful means they hold quite a power over us, especially if we are of the mindset that we "never have enough time" or "never have enough money." They are also powerful adversaries because our need for them brings particularly poignant emotions to the surface. If I say to you, for example, that you will lose time or lose money, how does that feel? Scary and upsetting, no doubt. It might even make you angry, frustrated, or worse, despondent and desperate. We fear the loss of time and money perhaps more strongly than we should. Nonetheless, fear is the dominant emotion.

Once again, it comes back to fear, doesn't it? And that's why we started there.

With time and money, the fears we saw earlier turn into the following thoughts:

- *I'm worried it will take too long.*
- *I don't have the time to do this well.*
- *I don't have the time to do this at all.*
- *I don't want to waste time on something that feels so risky and uncertain.*
- *I don't know how to make money from a book.*
- *I've heard authors don't make money or can't profit from books.*
- *I don't want to do all this work and waste all this time only to fail at it.*
- *I don't know how to get paid as an author once I write the book.*
- *Isn't publishing a book really expensive? I'll be in this too deep to get an ROI.*
- *I need money now; therefore, I don't have time to sit and write a book.*

Can you feel the powerful pull the desire for more time and more money have on us? Not only are we keenly aware of protecting the time and money we have right now, but we are also hungry to save our time and money and get more by any means possible. While this may not be apparent to you right away, I would like for you to think back to the last time you thought about sitting down to write your book. What got in your way? What were the thoughts you were having? List them below or in a notebook.

My thoughts about sitting down to write: _____

_____

Now that you've done that, can you see how your thoughts relate back to one or more of the Mental Adversaries of time, money, and fear? Can you see that the resistance to writing is a well-orchestrated offense by the brain to keep you safe, to protect you from perceived risk and failure? Can you sense how these thoughts feel in your body even as you sit here reading this? They don't feel good, relaxing, or comforting, do they? They don't feel peaceful. They feel like tension. They feel like resistance.

That resistance is something to pay attention to because it shows that, deep down, you do not want the Mental Adversaries to win. You actually do want—and probably need—to write your book. Why do I say *need*? Because the key to getting what you desire (more time and money in your life) comes from writing and publishing your book in the first place! That's the irony. The things you desire in life will arrive when you do what you are most afraid of, not when you avoid it.

That's why you must learn how to conquer these Mental Adversaries and move beyond them, so you can write and publish a book you can be proud of. The key to conquering your Mental Adversaries is to face the biggest of them all head-on. That's right, we must rid ourselves of fear and embrace a newfound sense of courage and confidence with our writing.

ADDRESSING FEAR HEAD-ON

In my early days of coaching, I had an author student whom we'll call Lisa. Lisa was, on paper, the perfect, qualified person to write a book. If you had presented her book idea to a publisher and shown them what she had done in her life and her many accolades, they would have snapped her up in no time flat. The problem was she was stuck and couldn't write her book.

Lisa had a hard time staying focused. She was a skilled writer, but every time she would sit down to write, a crisis would always come up. Her daughter would call with some urgent need, or a water pipe would burst, or a client would phone her and let her know of some catastrophe that simply couldn't wait. Lisa was forever distracted by crises that would show up, seemingly on demand.

On top of this, she was highly self-critical. When we had finished planning her book and she was ready to sit down to write, the words trickled out like a leaky faucet. Lisa grew frustrated and unhappy with herself. She would feel guilty and depressed for not writing and finally will herself back to the manuscript only to eke out a few words that she'd scrutinize deeply. Then she would freeze up and stop writing, and the cycle would repeat once more.

Sound familiar?

It wasn't long before I noticed how much Lisa was struggling with what I call the start-stop cycle. One day, during one of our coaching sessions, I stopped our tactical conversation and turned her attention to something else entirely.

Lisa had finished discussing all the reasons why she hadn't written since the last time we met. I could sense more was afoot and asked her a simple question: "Why do you really think you are not writing, Lisa?"

Lisa paused and looked at me. At first, she was rather taken aback, but I also knew she appreciated being pushed and challenged. After a few moments of excuses, Lisa had out with it: "I suppose I'm terrified," she said solemnly.

Saying it out loud was the first step in taking out her sword and waging a battle against those Mental Adversaries. I could tell something had shifted for her and that by acknowledging the fear she was feeling, she felt freer and ready to tackle her fear head-on. And tackle it she did. After that session, Lisa went on to finish writing her book in a few short weeks. She then embraced publishing, and we helped her create a powerful marketing campaign that launched her book to #1 bestseller status on Amazon. Because of her content and ability to attract other influential readers, Lisa was offered the opportunity to write more books and soon became an author for a second time. She's now being recognized in her field as a consultant and earning double what she was earning when we first began working together.

Conquering fear is powerful and necessary. When you conquer your inner fears about writing, you also do away with the more cursory Mental Adversaries of time and money. That's because fear is at the root of everything. Fear of failure. Fear of embarrassment. Fear of wasting time or losing money. It all boils down to our fearful feelings and our need to keep ourselves safe.

When I started tackling the mental side of writing in my work, success rates for my authors soared. I knew this was important work, but I also knew it would be complex work. That's because fear can show up in a multitude of ways and has the unique quality of appearing like logic. That is, we think something logical and assume there is no fear involved. For example, "I can't write today because I'm too busy and I have other more important things on my to-do list." It sounds reasonable, right? Indeed, but hidden behind the cloak of logic is the pervasive and subtle fear that one's work is not important enough or even worthy of prioritizing. Not only is this impractical, because we will all have busy days when writing could get pushed aside, but it is insidious, because it allows fear to run the show and decide whether or not your book gets written.

Let me give you another example of fear disguising itself as logic. Have you ever made a key decision only to later second-guess yourself and come up with a whole list of reasons as to why the decision you made didn't make sense, wouldn't work, or would end in a bad result? This might be known as self-sabotage or rationalizing. Remember that the human brain is always looking to create meaning. We are meaning-making machines! The brain is also always looking to keep us safe, so it's natural for the brain to come up with a list of seemingly rational reasons as to why your decision must be reversed.

In this case, fear of the unknown, or what might happen if you make the decision, is running the show, but the brain is very good at breaking that down and delivering a nice handy box of rational reasons for you to convince yourself not to move forward in order to keep you safe. Sometimes this is useful, and we can thank our survivalist brain, especially if our decision is to do something stupid like leap off a tall building. But it's less likely to be helpful when what we are doing is not a threat to our lives, like writing a book. We can see how annoying and unhelpful our survivalist brain is when it's delivering a nice box of fear-based rational when all we are trying to do is sit down and write the book we want to write. Thanks a lot, brain!

When fear causes our survivalist brain to react and starts dictating our actions, we write from a place of fear, not from a place of faith and trust in ourselves and in our work. This matters for two very important reasons. Firstly, when we write from a place of fear, we create psychological suffering for ourselves, and that suffering usually carries into our work and can be felt in the words that make it to the page. It's easy to tell, isn't it, when writing flows well and the writer seems to be enjoying the task at hand? Equally, when writing doesn't flow so well, when it is painful and arduous to get through, we feel it. Therefore, on some level, our psychological suffering can create an unpleasant experience for our readers if we let it.

Secondly, fear is usually caused by a lack of certainty, or the unknown ahead. We fear what we do not know or understand, and the human brain has a hard time dealing with uncertainty or the unknown. We like to make meaning out of things and search for experiences and evidence that support those meanings. When the outcome is unknown and we lack certainty, we begin to feel fear, and the psychological suffering begins.

So how do we deal with fear and conquer it once and for all? The first step is to acknowledge that you have some level of fear working against you. If you can dig deep enough to see that the reasons you're held back from writing ultimately stem from a very primal source of fear (fear of failure, fear of rejection, fear of not being good enough, etc.), then you can see fear for what it really is: simply your brain trying to avoid what it perceives as dangerous and keep you safe. The second step is to figure out what you're actually afraid of and put it into words. I invite you to do a short exercise. Sit down with a pen and a blank sheet of paper. In the center, write down your book idea and then circle it. Next, stemming from the circle, write down all the reasons why you have not been writing consistently. See if you can identify any patterns. See if you can see through those reasons to notice what is really lurking below the surface. Do you see your true fear? Have you found it yet?

Now for the final step. Once you see and acknowledge your fear, you have an opportunity to shift your focus and change your mindset. You do not have to allow fear to dictate what you do in your life! What I want you to see is that the most powerful decisions you make, the ones that will reshape your life and your destiny for the better, are those that involve confronting your fear and doing what you desire in spite of it. The moment you can do this and break free, the moment you see the fear and take action anyway, is the moment you develop courage.

Courage is not a talent, nor is it an inherent personality trait. Courage is a muscle, one you must exercise every single day. When you write and pursue your goals in spite of your fears, you exercise your courage muscle. The more you exercise it, the stronger it gets. If you want to be a successful, accomplished author, you must develop a strong courage muscle.

Thankfully, there is a powerful mindset technique to help you shift your focus and write from a place of courage, confidence, and focus much more easily. What is this powerful mindset technique, and how do we cultivate it for ourselves to combat fear, in all its forms? That is exactly the subject of the next chapter.

ACCESS THE CODE: COMBAT FEAR AND GET UNSTUCK

Are you stuck with your book right now? Here's an opportunity to grab my Get Unstuck Cheat Sheet that will help you get moving on your book quickly. Visit

www.writingcoachla.com/thecode
to access it along with further free reader resources.

CHRIS REAVIS

My experience with Ashley and her team was absolutely epic on so many fronts.

I knew I always had a story inside me, and I knew that if I could get that story out, I could help so many other parents like me. My son was born with autism, making school especially difficult, and quite honestly, parenting too.

After doing tons of research, I found a brain-based approach I knew I had to share with other parents. As important as my mission was, my fears, anxiety, and imposter syndrome nearly stopped me in my tracks. But Ashley's program and her team helped me address these head-on and provided so many practical steps to get my manuscript written, professionally edited, and finally published.

My book hit #1 bestseller status on Amazon in over ten categories thanks to the expertise of Ashley and her team. It has now helped me reach over 100,000 parents like me as well, thanks to the additional programs I could then build around my book. And, while that certainly came with revenue, it's knowing that my story has served others that is the most meaningful aspect of this journey by far.

I took what I learned from Ashley and used it to write and publish two more books to equal bestseller success and used them for additional program framework support. What she teaches is not some "one shot" deal—these lessons and practices really stick. It's honestly hard to believe how well it works.

I say this in the humblest way possible: I've now earned multiple six figures with my first two books and the programs around them, and I am on target to do the same with my third book.

This would not have happened without the expertise of Ashley and her team.

If you have a story, if you know you want to get it out there, and you know you also want to make money doing it, I am living proof that Ashley's programs work—three times in a row!

—CHRIS REAVIS, bestselling author of *Unleashed, Hashrate,* and
Boost Your Bullsh*t Resilience at Work

Shift Your Mindset from Craft to Strategy and the Words Will Flow

CHAPTER FIVE

The 3rd Secret

Shift Your Mindset from Craft to Strategy and the Words Will Flow

U P UNTIL NOW, you've been taught about the Mental Adversaries and the experience of fear as a first-time writer. But what I haven't given you yet is the magic elixir, which will help you adopt a powerful frame of mind while you write your book now and for every book you write in the future.

So, what is the magic elixir? It is the thing you need to understand if you're ever going to shift out of fear and self-doubt, procrastination, and writer's block.

You need to understand the number one mental shift that is absolutely essential for you to make if you ever want to finish a book in your lifetime.

Yes, it's that important. This mental shift is what is responsible for the tiny percentage, the 1 percent of people who actually write a book and get it published. These happy few have made this mental shift for themselves. When you understand the mental shift, you can ensure that once you start writing, you can finish your book.

No one sits down with the intention of never finishing their book. It just sort of happens. One day, you wake up and the idea you started on five years ago has morphed into a long, unwieldy thing you cannot contain and don't know what to do with any longer. One day, you wake up and realize that the book you intended to write after high school or college never got done. Maybe you realize the book you started was never completed because you didn't put in the consistent time and effort required.

So now, here you are, wondering why it is that great writers throughout history have made writing and creating books look so darn easy. How do they do it? What's the secret?

Are you ready for the elixir? Open wide!

They shift their mental focus from craft mastery to strategy mastery.

That's right. **When you shift your mindset from craft to strategy, the words will flow.**

Craft mastery is thinking about how good your writing is. Strategy mastery is thinking about how your book will get done.

The mental shift here that's so important is the following:

From . . . "How good it is." (craft)

To . . . "How to get it done!" (strategy)

The next section of this book is dedicated to two practices you can use to help you make this crucial mental shift for yourself. I'm also going to show you how you can utilize a strategy-only focus to go further faster than you ever have before in your life. I have been laying the foundation throughout this entire book to give you not only the right mindset but the right strategy to write your books—not just the current book but every single one you ever want to create.

A STRATEGY FOCUS UNLOCKS YOUR CRAFT

When I first began formally coaching aspiring authors, I had an author student named Thelma, whom I mentioned earlier. Our engagement began with a phone call that felt a little stilted because of the noisy background coupled with Thelma's endearing Filipino accent. But I listened closely, because in Thelma's voice, I could hear something important: determination.

Thelma had an amazing story to tell, and she was determined to tell it. She signed up for my Book Accelerator® coaching program, and together we began working on her very first book. Everything was going smoothly—that is, until I realized that as a nonnative English speaker, Thelma had very little experience with writing in English.

At first, I was concerned, but I made sure to follow what I'd seen work before with other authors and taught Thelma to focus on her strategy—getting the book done—instead of worrying about her craft. She seemed to embrace this concept easily and even expressed relief at not having to worry about how good her writing was, or even whether or not it was correct. As she began writing—persistent, inspired, and motivated to tell her story of fleeing the Philippines and building a life with her husband, Florendo—her words began to flow.

What I saw next from Thelma was astounding.

Over the next few weeks, her writing began to subtly morph. It was unusual to say the least, and I began to question whether Thelma had secretly hired a ghostwriter. But when I asked her, it was apparent there was no ghostwriter involved. Thelma's skill with the written word was simply improving naturally. She was learning to master the craft, even though her primary focus had been on the strategy I taught her and not the craft at all.

This is an important phenomenon that occurs when one focuses on the right thing, the right aspect of the writing process. And that part is strategy.

THE CRAFT MINDSET VERSUS THE STRATEGY MINDSET

If I asked you to think about writing a book, I bet you would think about craft mastery first, not strategy. That's because craft mastery is how we are taught to think about writing. From a young age, as we grasp new words, phrases, grammar, and spelling, we are shown how to master the craft of our language. This education is usually the first thing people think about when they consider writing a book.

When you do a search for "how to write a book," articles and resources on the craft are the sort of thing you turn up. Advice and guidance about the craft of writing is the industry's main focus. "Focus on your craft and the rest will follow" seems to be the primary piece of advice for aspiring authors, especially if you are writing fiction or a memoir. Unfortunately, focusing only on mastering the craft of writing doesn't lead to the outcome of a finished book, nor does it actually provide you with the necessary tools and steps to become a successful author. This is what I didn't understand about writing books when I first started out. I believed that my success path hinged on my ability to write, my craft. But if that were true, aspiring authors everywhere could simply focus on improving their craft, and that would automatically allow them to finish life-changing books, get published, and become billionaires many times over like J. K. Rowling.

But this is not how one becomes a successful author. Focusing on the craft alone is not going to get you to where you want to go. In fact, it can take you further and further away from your goal if you're not careful. A craft-only focus is particularly unhelpful when you're trying to finish a book, because writing a book is a finite process, but developing and improving one's craft is a lifelong pursuit. Therefore, if we adopt a craft-only mindset when writing our books, it's likely they will never get done, because *we* will never be done improving our craft. It's a vicious cycle and one that I myself have been trapped in.

Do you remember my story of writing a book for three years, focused only on the craft, and it ending up in my shredder? I had unwittingly fallen into something I call the Craft Trap, and I spent years and years toiling away on a book, obsessing over mastering and improving my craft when I should have been focused on a strategy to get the book done and published. The Craft Trap is prevalent among first-time and more experienced authors. If you have fallen into the Craft Trap, you've likely spent years and years writing, tweaking, editing, and revising your book but never moving closer to your goal of getting it done. The Craft Trap is a dangerous place that has kept many aspiring authors stuck and frustrated with their books.

How can we know if we are truly in the Craft Trap? It's simple. If you are stuck in the Craft Trap, you will find that you experience some or all of the following:

- Writer's block
- Procrastination
- Starting and stopping
- Never getting started
- Never finishing
- Giving up partway through
- Feeling overwhelmed, discouraged, and doubtful
- Never taking action at all because of fear

So how do we break free of the Craft Trap?

The first step is to realize that while the craft is important, the truth is you need more than the craft to finish a great book and become a successful author. Craft mastery is only part of the equation. You must also master strategy.

Strategy is essential because it supports, strengthens, and stabilizes your craft. It is the necessary foundation you must have in place for the craft to flourish at all. Strategy gets you to your end goal, while craft keeps you trapped and spinning in a never-ending cycle of continuous critique and self-improvement. Again, don't misunderstand what I'm saying. We need some level of craft. Of course we do! No one wants to write a bad book. The point, however, is that craft mastery alone cannot be our sole focus when we are trying to finish a book and get it published.

That's why the second step to break free from the Craft Trap is to shift your focus from craft to strategy. Strategy is the missing piece for everyone stuck in writer's block, procrastination, self-doubt, fear, over-whelm—all of it! And yet we are never taught about strategy, only the craft. But strategy is essential, because without it, you cannot tap into the creative power you really have, and you cannot evolve into the great writer you were born to be!

Let me be clear: you cannot get to the end goal of a finished bestsell-ing book with craft alone. At some point, if you have a book idea and you want to get it written, published, and in the hands of readers who will care, you *must* have a strategy.

A strategy focus will change everything for you. Once you have the end goal of your book in mind, you can take practical steps every day toward that goal and make real progress on what you most want to create. As you build momentum, you'll develop greater levels of courage and confidence that will ignite new abilities within you. In other words, you will unconsciously improve your craft while you focus solely on your strategy. The key is to stay in this strategy focus as much as possible while working on your book and avoid falling back into the Craft Trap, where you start worrying about your writing ability again. The moment you start thinking craft-focused thoughts, you must recognize it and, with that new awareness, go back to the strategy at hand.

What are craft-focused thoughts? Well, they are the thoughts aspir-ing authors most think:

- *Writing is really hard and takes considerable time.*
- *Writing is like opening a vein and bleeding out the words.*
- *I'm not a good writer. I can't string a sentence together.*
- *What if my story isn't good enough?*
- *What if I'm not good enough?*
- *I'm worried the book won't be good enough / won't turn out as I imagined / will be bad.*
- *What if I can't get it published? Then what will I do?*
- *I'm not really qualified to write / a "real" writer.*

- *Who am I to write this book?*
- *Everything I'm saying has been said before already. What's the point?*

Can you see how all of these thoughts eventually come back to craft and judgment about how good the writing is? That's what is so sneaky about the Craft Trap. We've been taught that this is the way to think about our books and our writing, that if we focus on the craft mastery, the words will flow and everything will come together. But if we focus on the craft mastery, all we will have is mastery of the craft. But darn it if there are not millions upon millions of skilled, qualified, brilliant writers out there desperate to write and be published who have never had a single book get out there. Why is that? Because as I have mentioned, a craft focus is not and cannot be your sole focus. You must have a way to get to the end goal of a published book that reaches your readers. And for that, you must have a strategy.

When you do utilize a strategy, these are the types of experiences you can expect:

- Clear goals and outcomes—clarity!
- The ability to commit and a "no excuses" mentality
- Alignment with your purpose for writing
- Focus (eliminate the distraction of the craft)
- Unshakable accountability
- The ability to take action despite risk or fear because of the focus on the end goal
- Improvement of your craft over time
- Faster, better, and more joyous writing
- A feeling of being "in the zone" of the writing
- A feeling of being free, happy, and at peace

These are the experiences I and my fellow authors have had when we have followed this approach, broken free from the Craft Trap, and learned to focus on strategy instead. I want the same for you. I want you to feel so empowered, so confident, so free while writing that the inner critic takes a long vacation and is reluctant to return to your mindscape. I want you to be so happy and joyous while writing that the words pour out of you as easily as they ever have, just as they did for Thelma, who went on to write two bestselling memoirs, speak in schools as a published author, and raise money for children's charities with her writing.

I want you to feel a sense of pride in your work, in its value and quality, and live in the space where anything is possible because you have imagined it to be so and used a proven strategy to help you get there.

But what strategy should you use?

I'm so glad you asked! The strategy I use for my own books, which I teach every single one of my aspiring authors, is called the TAP Method. It stands for the three essential things (time, accountability, and process) that every aspiring author needs to master in order to write a great book, publish it, and ultimately succeed in their endeavors. In the next chapter, we dive deeper into the first part of this essential book writing strategy and learn how to apply it to your own book to get it done and published faster than you ever thought possible.

ACCESS THE CODE: MASTER YOUR MINDSET

I created a short video training on mindset mastery for authors that I know will help you develop the right mindset to succeed. To access it in the reader resources section of my website, visit
www.writingcoachla.com/thecode

MARIA PIANTANIDA

I was a first-time author who dreamed of writing a book about my field of expertise but always felt uncertain about how to even get started down that path. I had no idea how to begin the process of writing a book, which meant I let way too many years pass before deciding to get serious about doing it.

I made the decision to consult with Ashley about my goals after speaking with another new author who had already joined Ashley's Book Accelerator® program and was loving it. Ashley gave me all the confidence and clarity I needed to dive in. With the TAP Method, I wrote my book in less than 90 days! Ashley's program and her incredible team guided me through every step with clarity and ease, making it truly painless to write a book from idea to finished draft. That meant I could actually enjoy being a writer without worrying about all the details that can be so confusing to someone who has never walked that path. I honestly can't wait to write my next book.

After finishing my book, I joined her Bestseller Legacy publishing program and became a full-fledged published author less than six months later! Not to mention, my book became a #1 bestseller on Amazon within the first few days of its release. Becoming a bestselling author has been such a fulfilling process; it's a bucket list endeavor that I've completed long before I ever dreamed I would. Joining Ashley's programs enabled me to realize just how enjoyable writing and publishing can truly be, and I loved every minute of the entire process.

The work I do is even more satisfying now that I'm a published author. It's as if I speak to my patients in a different way. I have always been very compassionate, but after writing, editing, and publishing a book about my work and personal experiences, it's almost as if I've realized my own credibility even more. I feel even better equipped to help those who are going through their own struggles, and that translates into how I work with them every day.

—MARIA PIANTANIDA, psychiatric mental health nurse
practitioner and bestselling author of *The Simple Art
of Getting Unstuck*

SARAH ALSERHAID

Writing and publishing my first book was an immensely rewarding personal achievement. I work as a scientist in women's health, so having written and published a fictional magical realism book is always quite the conversation starter! And the personal growth I experienced throughout the process was mind-blowing.

As a fiction writer in Ashley's Book Accelerator® and Publishing Master programs, I was able to take the lessons and advice given and work it into my own writing journey in a way that made complete sense for my book. I finished my manuscript and went through a great revision process with my editor while the rest of Ashley's team put together a publishing proposal, landing me a publishing deal!

I combined the very best of Ashley's notes and my editor's notes to result in a final book that was so beautiful. I was able to secure endorsements for it from award-winning authors, and my book was even shortlisted for an award for its cover design. It was released to great reviews, and I already have two sequels underway that my publisher has committed to launching as well.

This has been such an incredible and rewarding journey that is only just beginning, and I'm not sure I would have ever made it here without Ashley and everything she does.

—SARAH ALSERHAID, bestselling author of *Etched in Stone*

BECOME A MASTER OF TIME

CHAPTER SIX

THE 4TH SECRET

Become a Master of Time

THE COLDEST AND HOTTEST I've ever been in my entire life was on the Mediterranean island of Malta. During the three years I was there, I experienced the harshest winters, the most raging summers, and this other phenomenon called island time. Every foreigner knew about island time. Island time meant that things happened a little slower than you were used to and you had to be patient. *Really* patient. Back then, patience wasn't my virtue, and while the rest of the island seemed to have all the time in the world, I had none of it.

At the time, I was working long hours, getting into the office before everyone else and leaving after everyone else. I'd spend twelve or fourteen hours in the office, go home, eat a quick dinner, and then get back on my laptop for another few hours of work until it was so late I couldn't keep my eyes open anymore. I was a workaholic, throwing myself into the daily grind in a way that was unsustainable and unhealthy. Beneath my extreme work ethic was a burning desire to become an author. Through late nights and early mornings at this job, my own dream of becoming a published author lingered on.

With my busy schedule running my life, I wondered where I was going to get the time to write my book. I realized I couldn't make more time, I could only use the time I had more efficiently. I knew deep down that I needed to get in control of my time and that my experience of it—never having enough—was somehow within my control. The Maltese seemed to have an abundance of time, remember. They never seemed to be in a hurry, rushing around late and delayed. They didn't freak out about getting things done or not having enough time to do what they wanted to. On the contrary. The Maltese seemed to feel they had an abundance of time—more than they needed each and every day—and when things got done, they got done. It was very strange to me indeed!

One day, I decided I would try this mentality with my book. What if I could change my thinking to believe that I had more than enough time to write it? What if I could be like the Maltese and simply sit back, be patient, and enjoy the journey? Could I actually change my perception of time and somehow magically create the hours I needed to write? I was willing to give it a shot.

This was important to me because I had seen other successful writers, and all of them seemed to have a very good and clear relationship with time. They were not like me, hurried and rushing around, doing everything except writing. Because time was the first part of the equation, I knew I needed to master it, and I was willing to put in the work to do that, especially if it meant my book could get done and I could accomplish my goal of becoming a published author.

How about you? Are you willing to put in the work to master time and achieve your goals? If your relationship with time is a lot like mine was, then you'll want to read on to learn the time mastery principles I'm going to teach you so that you can improve your relationship with time and master this important factor.

HOW TO MASTER TIME

If your relationship with time is a lot like mine was, chances are you feel you never have enough time to do the things you need to do, let alone the things you *want* to do—like write your book! Most people believe they cannot possibly fit writing a book into their busy lives and schedules.

They fear it will take too long, that it will be impossible to finish in a timely manner. The reason people usually resort to this limited way of thinking is simple. What I've found is that most people vastly overestimate how long a book should take to write. This is especially true for first-time authors, who typically spend far too much time on the first draft. They may spend years or even decades working on a single project, toiling away but never feeling momentum or real progress. This is such a shame and one of the great tragedies I see as a book coach. I always hate to see someone struggle with their unfinished book for years and never get it done, let alone published. When they do release the book, often it's a product they don't feel proud of, and they still worry it isn't good enough. This happens to first-time authors every single day. It's no wonder the experience of clinging so tightly to their books and then releasing them with a fraction of the thought and dedication that they poured into writing them yields this sad result.

But it doesn't need to be this way!

There is a solution, and it's simpler than you might think.

The solution starts with understanding exactly how long writing a book should take you.

Up until now, there has never been a formula for people to figure out how long writing a book should actually take. If you don't believe me, do a Google search right now. You'll see a plethora of answers ranging from a few days to a year, a few years, or even longer! Ultimately, every resource you look at will tell you that it depends on the writer and the book.

Gee, thanks a lot, you may be thinking. And you're right to think that, because the information out there isn't very helpful. It's probably more helpful today than it was when I first began my writing journey, because of people like me trying to make it simpler, but the fact remains that the only place you're going to find a formula like I'm about to teach you is right here.

THE TIME MASTERY FORMULA

So there I was, working long, crazy hours, living on vending machine food and pizza, trying to figure out how I could make the time I needed to write my book. The cool thing was that in my job, I had learned some pretty awesome things from the producers at our company, who used an agile development process called Scrum to help them schedule projects and get them done on time as well as understand how to plan ahead to make sure all the factors would be covered. I knew I needed to have something similar and act as a producer of sorts for my own project, which was this new book I was going to write. I decided early on that I would create a formula around time like the formulas I'd seen these producers use to bring speed, efficiency, and consistent momentum to the projects they were overseeing. I got to work on the formula and found that the first thing I needed to understand was my own writing speed.

DISCOVER YOUR WRITING SPEED

Knowing your writing speed is the first and most important part of the Time Mastery Formula. Most people don't have a clue how fast they actually write. If you ask them, they will give you all sorts of answers ranging from a number of pages and paragraphs to chapters and sections. But very few people measure writing speed correctly.

The truth is we measure writing speed the same way we do driving a car. When we're driving, we measure speed in miles per hour. When we're writing, we measure speed in words per hour. The reason we use words per hour is because we need to understand what we, the writers, can produce (the number of words) in a single unit of time (one hour). Additionally, in the book world, editors and publishing professionals reference the length of books by the number of words they contain. They do not usually reference pages because that is a number that can change depending on the typesetting and book's design. A larger font means more pages, while a smaller font means fewer pages. The total word count, however, is always a fixed number.

The appropriate total word count for your book is important to know in order to figure out how long the book will actually take you to write—that is, the total number of writing hours. When we know this, we can start to plug it into our schedules and create realistic goals for getting it done. This is exactly what I did to make sure I could actually finish writing my book in a reasonable period of time. I do this same exercise every time I set out to write a book.

Knowing your writing speed in words per hour is very valuable because it's going to give you clarity on what you can do with an hour (how much writing you can produce), a benchmark to work from and improve upon, as well as perspective on the whole book. Understanding your speed will help you break down the book into bite-sized chunks that you can manage to tackle every single day. How do you eat an elephant? One bite at a time.

To discover your words per hour (WPH) writing speed, the first thing you need to do is a short freewriting exercise. In case you are unfamiliar with freewriting, it is a simple technique where you simply sit down to write without worrying about the craft. That means no correcting your spelling, or your grammar, and no going back to overthink or edit what you have written. You simply write and let the words flow out of you. My author students usually find this type of writing immediately freeing, exciting, and wonderful. Some have a bit of hesitation going in because they've been taught to edit and revise while they write and have trouble letting the imperfection stand on the page. With practice, however, they find that freewriting is a freeing and wonderful experience. There is another reason I'm teaching you to write like this that relates to the first draft, but we'll cover that in more depth in chapter 10.

Coming back to your exercise, the goal here is to freewrite about your book topic to discover your words per hour (WPH) writing speed.

The first thing you must do before you start is make sure your writing area is free of distractions and noise. Create your optimal writing environment and remove any temptation to do anything except write. I like to put my phone on do-not-disturb mode, let my family know I'm going to be writing for an hour, put on my noise-canceling headphones, and turn the internet off. This is my practice, and it may not be possible for you to do all of this, but you at least want to be in a quiet and focused environment.

Next, set a timer for thirty or sixty minutes. If this is the first time you are freewriting, I would highly recommend starting this exercise with thirty minutes. For some people, this can feel like a very long time to write continuously. With practice, though, it will get easier, and you will work up to forty-five and sixty minutes. If you are used to writing and already have a writing habit, you can shoot for the full sixty minutes. Put your timer on and freewrite about your book topic for the full thirty or sixty minutes without stopping. Remember, no editing and no going back, just put the words down.

When the timer dings, you can check the total number of words you have written. By the way, you can do this exercise writing longhand or typing on your computer (or typewriter, if that's what floats your boat). The only caveat here is that you should complete this exercise using the method of writing you plan to use to write your entire book in order for it to be accurate. I recommend typing on a computer for that reason. Also, it's a lot easier to count the number of words you have written in a word processor than it is longhand or typewriting. This is a feature all word processors have, and you should check your particular software provider for instructions.

Got it? Now that you're done, go ahead and count those words. Can you see where I'm headed with this?

If you wrote for a full sixty minutes, congratulations—you've discovered your WPH writing speed. If you wrote for thirty minutes, multiply the number by two to get your WPH writing speed.

For example, if you wrote for 60 minutes and your word count is 1,250 words, your WPH is 1,250 words per hour.

If you wrote for 30 minutes and your word count is 550 words, your WPH is 1,100 words per hour.

How did you do? Is the number surprising? Most people who do this exercise for the first time are a little uncertain about their results. They don't really know if their number is good or bad, high or low. So let me give you some parameters to better understand the number.

I see a lot of writing speeds, and after helping so many authors—hundreds now—I know the average WPH writing speed for most people is about 1,000 WPH. So, the good news is if you are at this threshold or faster, you're in a great place. If you're below this mark, it might be because you are handwriting or typing slowly or because you are overthinking. In all my years of doing this work, the thing I see most frequently is overthinking. Even those who handwrite their entire books or are slower at typing can eventually reach 1,000 WPH, especially if they use a technique I'm going to teach you later in this book. So, if you are typing and you're not at 1,000 words per hour yet, that's okay! It takes practice to build up your speed and get your words out of your head and onto the page. Don't be too hard on yourself if you are writing more slowly. Simply repeat the exercise, this time with a deep breath, a little meditation and relaxation before you start, and see if you can get out of your head and into the zone of writing freely, without second-guessing yourself.

Freewriting is all about allowing the words to come out without the voice of the inner critic judging you. If you're slower than 1,000 words per hour, and you are typing well and do not have a physical limitation that prevents you from typing, then chances are your inner critic is slowing you down. This is a good opportunity to notice this and do something about it before we go deeper. My advice would be to practice freewriting and notice what your inner critic is saying. As I joke with my author students, you can send that inner critic on a long vacation to the Bermuda Triangle where they are likely to get lost and never return, because the inner critic isn't going to be useful for a long, long time. So let's get that plane ticket and suitcase ready for them. That way, you can repeat your freewriting and discover your average writing speed, or how fast you normally write.

AVERAGE WRITING SPEED

I've just touched upon something important—the average writing speed. I recommend repeating the WPH exercise three or four times and creating an average WPH writing speed. Take all your test word counts from each session, add them up, and divide the sum by the number of hours you wrote. This will give you an average. Why does this matter? Because some days you will be super fast and feeling great, and other days you may be slower. I don't want you to feel alarmed when you are. Remember that the words will flow at their own pace, and you will tend to fall into the bracket of your own average writing speed. If you know what that is, you can manage yourself and your mindset so much better.

ADJUSTED WRITING SPEED

Something all my author students create is what I call an adjusted writing speed. After they find their average WPH writing speed, I have them slow it down by about 25 percent. The reason is that I want them to have a buffer. A buffer is important because it gives you a little breathing room for your project. That little extra space in your time budget can be surprisingly helpful and will help you stay on track. You'll see why in a moment, but for now, go ahead and reduce your writing speed by 25 percent. Here's a quick example.

Let's say your writing speed is 1,200 WPH. To slow that down by 25 percent, multiply 1,200 by 0.25 and you get 300.

Next, subtract 300 from 1,200 and you get 900. Your adjusted speed is 900 WPH.

Let's say you are writing a 40,000-word book. As you will see in a moment when I reveal the entire Time Mastery Formula, writing that book at 900 WPH will take you 44.4 total hours, versus 33.3 hours writing at 1,200 WPH. This means you have built in a time buffer with your adjusted writing speed of about eleven hours.

Again, the formula for calculating your adjusted writing speed looks like this:

Average WPH Writing Speed X 0.25 = 25 Percent Buffer
Average WPH Writing Speed – 25 Percent Buffer = Adjusted WPH Writing Speed

Now let's see how all of this fits into the Time Mastery Formula itself. If you use this formula, you will not only gain a greater mastery of time, but you should expect to have an aha moment of surprise when you realize just how fast you can write your book.

THE TIME MASTERY FORMULA REVEALED

Now that you have the basics down, it's time to get more granular with the Time Mastery Formula. Remember, the formula will help you understand approximately how long the book should take you to write. Right now, you may be overestimating how many hours you are going to need to write your book. In your mind, is the elephant you are eating the size of Mount Rushmore? If so, that's totally normal, but if we can plug in some actual numbers, like your writing speed, the elephant is going to shrink down to a little toy-sized Dumbo.

The Time Mastery Formula you're going to need to remember is:

Target Word Count / WPH = Total Writing Hours

We've already broken down how to obtain your average and adjusted WPH writing speed. So the only other number we need is your target word count. Let's fill in the gap right now.

The target word count is basically how many total words you are shooting for in your book. Many novice writers and aspiring authors sit down to start writing without knowing what this number should be. Despite what you might be led to believe by creative writing courses and other craft-focused schools, you cannot simply write the book without a clear word count goal or make it "as long as it needs to be." I used to really dislike it when people would ask, "How long should the book be?" and people would answer with something vague like, "As long as it needs to be to tell the story." First of all, that is a terrible answer because, in case you didn't know, you can tell the same story in as many words as you like. Take the story of Moses. You could tell it in a picture book, a short chapter book for older kids, a novel for young adults, or a long book series for adult readers. There is no appropriate length for that story, is there?

Yet this is the kind of advice out there that steers many first-time authors the wrong way. You need to understand exactly how long your book should be (the target word count), because doing so can make or break your book. We'll cover why and how in the next chapter.

ACCESS THE CODE: TIME MASTERY TRAINING

I created a short video training on time mastery for authors that I know you'll find helpful. To access it in the reader resources section of my website, visit
www.writingcoachla.com/thecode.

MATTHEW GREGER

I didn't start off with a dream of writing a book. I joined Ashley's 5-Day "Get Your Book Done" Boot camp out of curiosity, knowing that someday, having a book could benefit my business. As a certified high-performance coach helping people discover their brilliance, I wanted to see how writing a book could potentially fit into my coaching.

After joining the VIP Boot camp, I realized it was exactly what I needed. Ashley over-delivers on value and gives you more than expected. Afterward, I knew for sure that I had to write a book, but I also knew I needed help doing it, so I joined her Book Accelerator® program. My journey wasn't about the book itself, but the doors a book could open—gaining new opportunities by becoming a best-selling author. The book would be my "business card." I honestly didn't have a specific book idea from the start, but I had a clear mission, purpose, and the drive to get my story out there to serve and support my coaching business.

The Book Accelerator® program was powerful, but what I enjoyed most was the mindset coaching and support from the team. Ashley herself is a mindset coach, and I believe mindset is 90 percent of what you need to write a book. If you don't have the right mindset, nothing will help you get to the finish line. With the right mindset, it's all about mastery. That's where the TAP Method came in—mastering time, being accountable to myself and others, and, above all, trusting the process. That structure was invaluable. I went from no specific idea for a book to a completed first draft in just five months . . . wow! Handing it in felt fantastic! A monumental achievement.

I chose to stay with Ashley's team and publish with Brands Through Books because of their track record producing bestselling books. As a coach, I know the value of learning from someone with experience, so instead of wasting time figuring things out on my own or second-guessing every step, I trusted Ashley and her team to guide me through the process. They helped me reach milestones I hadn't even considered possible at the beginning of this journey! My book has exponentially uplifted my coaching business, enabling me to help so many people discover their brilliance!

—MATTHEW GREGER, mindset coach and bestselling author of *Think Brilliance*

CHAPTER SEVEN

WORD COUNTS:
The Magic Number

WHEN IT COMES to the total word count of your book, there is a magic number you should try to hit. And no, this number is not whatever number you magically land on while writing. Rather, this number is one that should be carefully thought about and planned from the get-go. You'll want to find this number at the start of the project and plan out how you're going to hit it before you put pen to paper. First-time authors who do this and stick to their goals have a far greater likelihood of 1) finishing the book and 2) getting it published quickly. Let's look at why.

REASON #1: EDITORS WON'T EDIT A BOOK OF ANY LENGTH.

At some point, you will need to work with an editor. No matter how many times you've self-edited, you still need a professional editor. You will find that editors are usually very discerning and disciplined people with very clear thinking and analytical minds. They will tell you flat out if your book is too long, and a great many of them will advise that you cut it down yourself to an acceptable length before working with them. If your book is too short, they will do the opposite and tell you to beef it up before you start working together. The other thing that is important to understand is that if you are paying an editor yourself and you have an oversized book, the cost to edit said book is going to be higher because editors usually charge by the word. So that's yet another good reason to stay within the limits of your target word count.

REASON #2: PUBLISHERS WON'T PUBLISH A BOOK OF ANY LENGTH.

The number of words publishers look for and expect to see from first-time authors has decreased over the years. It's now more acceptable than ever for nonfiction books to be about 40,000 to 50,000 words and for fiction to be around 70,000 to 80,000 words. I know publishers, for instance, that will balk at an 80,000-word novel as being on the long side. Of course, if you look online, you'll find plenty of examples of higher and lower word counts, but the point is you want to be in the sweet spot for what the majority of publishers are expecting and looking for if you ever plan to work with a publisher. If you don't and you want to self-publish, you may have more flexibility, but you'll still want to be mindful of the word count for two other reasons.

REASON #3: READERS WON'T READ A BOOK OF ANY LENGTH.

Remember that you need to write a book others will read. Otherwise, what's the point, right? Your readers will have certain expectations of your book depending on which genre you are writing in. These are called genre conventions. The best way to go about understanding these conventions is to look at other books published in your space to get an idea of what other successful first-time authors have done. What you'll find is that some genres are expected to be shorter or longer than others. For example, fantasy fiction for adults and young adults is typically much longer than contemporary romance or mystery. Equally, self-development and self-help books are usually shorter than some of the medical health and wellness books that have extensive sections related to treatments, conditions, or wellness protocols. It's not a hard-and-fast rule, but you're looking to fit into your own category and genre, not stand out—at least not when it comes to your target word count. The best way to find your magic word count number is to research other competitive titles in your space and genre that sold well in the past five years. This will help you determine about how long your book should be.

To find the appropriate target word count for your book, you need to understand the average length of books in your genre. A genre is simply a category or type of book. Romance is a genre. Sci-fi is a genre. Self-help is a genre. Business is a genre. You can have primary genres and smaller category-level genres that are really specific. Amazon uses genres to categorize books in its retail lists and niches them into specific categories like women's spiritual growth, marketing and sales, or medical textbooks. There are thousands of different categories out there but only a few big genres to consider for your book. For now, you need to develop a good understanding of what your primary genre is and then build a list of competitive titles based upon this.

This can be a quick exercise done online. Pull up your browser and search for books you believe are most like yours that have good reviews and were published in the last five years. Try to find bestsellers in your genre so you know they sold well. If you don't know of any, search for generic terms like "books about [my topic]." You'll get a whole bunch of competitive titles right away. You can then check out Amazon, Barnes & Noble, your local bookstore or library, and sites like Goodreads.com to see how these books are categorized and what the primary genre seems to be. When you have the primary genre, write it down and build a list of three to five competitive titles for your book.

Next up, do a simple Google search to find the word counts for each comp. You can type something like "word count of [book title]." You should see some results because many sites are now tracking the total word count of books that have been published. If you don't find your competitive titles, don't worry. Keep searching for other popular titles in your genre and category and gather their word counts instead.

If word counts for your competitive titles are not available, you can also do a little quick math and calculate the total competitive titles yourself. For example, single-spaced printed books have about 500 words per page, while double-spaced books have about 250 words per page. You can multiply these figures by the number of pages in your comp book to get an approximate word count for that specific book. For example, a 200-page book that is double-spaced would be 250 x 200 or 50,000 words long.

When you have word counts for three to five various comp books, you can find the average. This should give you a ballpark total word count to shoot for. Once you have this ballpark total word count, you can check it against your desired result (working with a publisher or self-publishing) and see if it works well for you. For example, let's say I'm writing a leadership book and I get a ballpark total word count from my competitive titles research of about 60,000 words. Maybe my goal is to self-publish and I don't want the book to be that long because of the cost of editing. So instead, I'll shoot for 50,000 words. See how this works?

Ultimately, you get to decide, but it's a good idea to make an informed decision and bank on a number that is going to be something editors will edit, publishers will publish, and readers will read.

Next up, take your target word count and plug it into the Time Mastery Formula we discussed in the previous chapter. Let's take a business and leadership book that's 40,000 words long and plug it in. Here is the formula one more time:

Target Word Count / WPH = Total Writing Hours

40,000/WPH = Total Writing Hours

Now let's plug in the average writing speed of 1,250 WPH.

40,000/1,250 = 32 Total Writing Hours

What does this result mean? It means that to write a 40,000-word book at a writing speed of 1,250 WPH would take about 32 hours of writing time. Thirty-two hours isn't very much, is it? It's four eight-hour days of writing, or divided more sensibly for breaks and other tasks, it's about eight hours a week for four weeks! Not a terribly big elephant, right?

What if the writing speed was slower, however? Let's say 1,000 WPH, or the average for most people. That would make for forty hours of total writing time, about a workweek for most of us. It's really important to use this Time Mastery Formula right away because now that you have the answer, you can begin to control time instead of it controlling you.

When you master time, you can plug these hours into your schedule and make writing your book even easier! You do not have to sit down and write for all thirty-two or forty hours in a single sitting. Of course not! Although I bet one of my authors very soon will attempt something like this as they get faster and more determined!

But you certainly don't need to do that, and in fact, I'd advise that you break down the total writing hours exactly as we do in my Book Accelerator® 90-day writing program. In Book Accelerator®, we take aspiring authors through the entire writing process, from having the raw idea for a book all the way to the finished manuscript in 90 days (13 weeks). We spend the first five weeks on prewriting and planning using the TAP Method to build the foundation (prewriting, formal plans, etc.) for the book and teach the writing strategy to our author students. The fun part about our planning process that we don't tell authors until later (we keep it a surprise) is that all the planning work we do up front has a couple of key benefits. Namely, using our TAP Method prewriting and planning process ensures:

1. Their book will be more likely to get picked up by a publisher and become a bestseller when the time comes.
2. Their book will be more likely to attract readers and get positive reviews.
3. Their book will be easier to market and launch to a specific niche audience.

Pretty awesome, right? We don't stop here, though. After the five weeks of planning are up, we then have our budding authors write for a period of eight weeks exactly. We call this part of the program "accelerated writing" because the techniques we teach allow our students to write fast, write well, and often finish their books in as few as two to four weeks. On average, for a 40,000-word book written at about 1,000 words per hour, most of our author students spend only about 5 hours per week writing the book. Most of my author students schedule that into their weeks very easily, either sitting down for an hour every weekday morning or for a few hours over the weekend. And because we encourage them to accelerate their writing if they wish to, many authors write full-time and finish their books much faster. At the time of writing, our current record holders in Book Accelerator® completed their full-length books in just fourteen days!

Do you see how easy this can be when you really understand the Time Mastery Formula? It truly is a game-changer, not only because you're able to make incremental progress with your book but because you shift your thinking and get into a clear, powerful mindset knowing exactly what it will take to write your book. This is called creating predictability.

Predictability is very important for our brains, especially when we are starting something new and embarking on a journey into the unknown. Remember that uncertainty and unpredictability create fear and send us into flight, fight, or freeze. When we enter fight, flight, or freeze mode, we quickly become overwhelmed and want to give up or quit on our goals. You can see how such a state of being is not conducive to writing fast and writing well, can't you? When you're in fight, flight, or freeze mode, it's very hard to be creative and focus or find inspiration. In this state of being, your brain, clever as it is, will come up with a million excuses and reasons why you shouldn't write your book.

Predictability gives us comfort, security, and a sense of control. This is so important and can immediately erase all the fear, doubt, second-guessing, and procrastination that takes place. If I had to boil the majority of our authors' success down to a single principle, it would be this one: through mastering time, they have come to understand how powerful they are and what they are really capable of. The scary elephant that was the size of a mountain gets diminished to the size of a small molehill, and soon my author students are conquering the writing process faster than they ever thought possible.

Let's talk for a moment about what else time mastery does for you. Understanding the metrics I've taught you in this chapter will also help you create speed and efficiency in your writing. By speed, I mean literally writing faster—faster writing sessions, higher WPH writing speeds, and getting to your end goal sooner.

"But wait!" I hear you say. "I don't want to rush and write a bad book! I want to take my time."

I understand. But you need to know one thing: just because you take longer to write your book doesn't mean it's going to be better!

In fact, there is a sweet spot for writing a book of about two to four months. That's about how much time you should be spending on your first draft. When the first draft drags out longer, you become fatigued, de-energized, and disconnected from your material. The longer the book takes, the less likely you are to finish it for these reasons. This is why when you first begin writing, it's better to write faster and simply get it done.

The number one thing I hear my authors say when they complete our Time Mastery Training module in the TAP Method course is "I can do this!" And that's exactly why we start with time.

I want you to feel the same way. You can do this! Writing your book doesn't need to take you forever or be difficult. It can be fast, easy, and really fun! Remember, the aspiring authors who come to me have been struggling for years and even decades with their books, and they get them done, published, and out into the world faster than they ever thought possible using the Success Code I've been sharing with you. The people I work with don't have some magical writing ability or some secret superpower that makes them succeed. But what they do have is the ability to commit, decide, and take action. That's it! When they follow the steps, beginning with time mastery, everything changes for them really quickly. It can for you too!

TIA'S STORY

Tia was one of the busiest people I had ever met. Not only was she a business owner, a coach, and a professional speaker, but she was also a corporate consultant and homeschooled her two kids full-time. If anyone had zero time to write, it was Tia. She was constantly on the go, and between running her business, being a mom, and giving so much to others, I often wondered if the formula would really work for her too.

Before we got started, I remember Tia saying to me that she hoped what I would teach her would make writing feel easy. She was excited to become an author and write a book, but the whole venture was new territory for her. A gifted speaker, Tia was new to writing, and this was her first book.

A few weeks in, it became apparent Tia was going to do well and master time like a pro. She went on to finish her 45,000-word manuscript in 7 weeks. We then worked together to help her pitch her book to a list of her favorite publishers. Almost overnight, her dream publisher came back interested in her book. Tia was over the moon, and so was I. Her dreams were coming true, all because of a few short months of diligence with the TAP Method.

And Tia isn't alone. At the time of writing, I've had students write their books even faster. Like Karine, who wrote her book on emotional intelligence in six weeks. Or Steve, who completed his 100,000-word novel in 5 weeks. Or Nathan, who wrote his complete real estate book in three weeks! Or Morgan and Katelyn, who set a new record and finished their entire books in eighteen days each! Multiple students have completed entire full-length books in fourteen days, many of which have gone on to become bestsellers.

It's totally possible for you to do this too when you master time. When you complete the exercises I recommend to help you master time, you'll find that you have a whole new relationship with time and that your book project, which once felt daunting, long, and arduous, is suddenly more doable. You will feel a sense of empowerment over your book and a sense of control over time. Remember, that is the whole point. You either take control of time or time is always going to be in control over you. This is the first step toward putting a foundation in place for your writing that will not only help you complete a great book in a short amount of time but help you grow and develop yourself into the author you desire to be.

Mastering time is one thing. But what about staying accountable and seeing your book through to publication? In the next chapter, we'll take a look at the ways in which we misunderstand true accountability so that we can learn to become accountable to our books and show up consistently to write and publish them.

ACCESS THE CODE: DISCOVER THE MAGIC NUMBER

How long should your book be? I created a Word Count by Genre Cheat Sheet you can use to take the guesswork out of the equation. To access it in the reader resources section of my website, visit **www.writingcoachla.com/thecode**.

Author Success Story

TIFFANI BARTON

Working with Ashley and the team at LA Writing Coach was nothing short of amazing! If you're even thinking about writing a book for the first time, you will find no one better to guide you than Ashley. From start to finish in both her Book Accelerator® program and her Brands Through Books publishing program, the process was an absolute joy! Her team is reliable, trustworthy, and filled with creative energy. They were just as committed to making my dream come true as I was.

Using the TAP Method, I finished my manuscript in just twenty-three days—something I never thought possible! The experience was easier and far more enjoyable than I expected. The publishing process that came after was seamless and well-organized, thanks to a fabulous team that guided me every step of the way. It truly felt like a cocreation, and the book turned out even better because of the collaborative effort.

I'm incredibly proud of my book, especially since it tells a vulnerable, personal story that I can now share with authenticity. The best part? My book became an overnight bestseller on Amazon, which has been life-changing! Within just a few short weeks of its release, I was featured on multiple podcasts and also began receiving messages from readers about how my story has impacted them.

I also created my brand-new coaching program in just one hour based on my book's content! Writing and publishing a book was truly one of the best decisions I ever could have made for my business. A huge thank you to Ashley and the entire LAWC team! I couldn't have done it without you!

—TIFFANI BARTON, coach and founder of Inner Sovereign
and bestselling author of *SHED*

DIANTE FUCHS

With Ashley's Book Accelerator® program, I wrote a book in just four short weeks from start to finish, writing less than one hour per day. By following her TAP Method, I was able to write the entire thing without getting stuck or discouraged even once! It felt incredibly amazing. Getting the first draft done was such an important milestone that led to me being published and launching my book to the world. Thanks to the guidance of the TAP Method, I ended up receiving offers from not one but two different publishers. I couldn't believe it!

My book was published in September 2024 and it has been such an incredible and surreal experience to finally get here. My business is growing, and new readers are signing up for my courses and programs. Now that I have the TAP Method in my arsenal, there's nothing stopping me from writing even more books and feeling 100 percent confident about the journey.

Part of me still doesn't quite comprehend that I wrote a book, and one that publishers actually wanted. But here I am, and I never would have made it without Ashley and Book Accelerator®.

—DIANTE FUCHS, clinical psychologist and
bestselling author of *The Gift of Anxiety*

Become a Master of Accountability

CHAPTER EIGHT

CHAPTER EIGHT

THE 5TH SECRET

Become a Master of Accountability

KARINE THOUGHT she was being accountable. She'd show up on time or early for our sessions. She would complete the lessons and assignments as she was supposed to. She asked good questions, took diligent notes, and was always mindful of her actions. Karine was an excellent student, but she wasn't yet demonstrating true accountability.

Most of us misunderstand what it means to be accountable when it comes to writing a book. But this is important because accountability is the second part of the TAP Method (the *A* in TAP) and something we absolutely need to master. We think if we show up on time, exercise care and responsibility, and do the work, we are being accountable. Accountability equals responsibility, doesn't it? The problem is this is not the measure of true accountability. Regardless of what you might think, being accountable is not

- Being answerable to yourself and your goals.
- Being responsible for your business or your family.
- Checking off the things on your to-do list.
- Checking in with your work group or accountability partner.

We largely misunderstand what true accountability is and how one creates it in relation to writing a book. Most first-time authors tend to think of it in outward terms, for example, checking in, showing up on time, or meeting a deadline. But these behaviors are an outward expression of something much deeper that is the true measure of accountability.

When it comes to writing a book, true accountability means writing for the sake of something greater than yourself and fulfilling a mission or honoring a greater purpose. **Accountability means writing in service to your reader.**

So many people begin writing their books for themselves, without regard for their readers. And guess who they then end up being accountable to? Themselves, that's right. But when you understand this isn't real accountability but only surface-level accountability, you begin to build the real inner commitment you need to author a great book.

Let's go back to Karine. Needless to say, when I told her that she wasn't showing up for her reader, she was confused and a little irritated.

"How can this be?" she asked me. "I'm always here, I'm always working. I never quit."

"Yes, I know," I said to her. "But you are still writing this book for yourself."

Highlighting the language of her manuscript, I pointed out that she was writing as if the book were going to be read by her and only her. It was more of an internal monologue than a self-help book for someone else. It was clear she didn't yet have the reader in mind while writing.

After I pointed this out to her early on in the process, she got it. It was as though a lightbulb clicked on in her head. Not only did her writing take off, but everything else did too. She became steadfast in her mission, clearer in her goals, and even more determined in a way I'd never seen her. Most importantly though, she began to make decisions about the book according to what would serve the reader most, not simply based on what would serve her.

It's important that you make the same leap Karine did if you ever want to tap into the power of true accountability. If you're not showing up regularly for your book, if you lack motivation, or if you struggle to hold yourself accountable, it's likely because the only layer of accountability you have is to yourself, and for many of us, letting ourselves down is easier than letting someone else down.

It's also likely that you haven't yet discovered who your ideal reader is and how the book will serve them. Once you do, you will tap into a greater level of accountability, and it will be powerful. You will be able to write more consistently, express yourself in new ways on the page, and activate a level of determination that you never knew was inside of you.

Don't try to start or continue writing without this piece of the TAP Method in place. Accountability is so important because it's the glue that holds everything together. Without it, you can have all the rest of the strategy, but you'll never actually commit to your book going beyond you. Instead, you will always be writing and showing up for yourself, and for most people, it's too easy to simply *not* do that. It's too easy to say, "Not today. I'll do it some other time."

As I sit here writing these words, I write them for you, with you in mind. I want this book to help you, and I'm very clear on how these chapters will assist you reach your goals. I desire your success, and I crafted the contents of this book specifically for that purpose.

Whether you are a fiction writer or nonfiction writer, you must understand that it is often easier to write a book that isn't for you and you alone. It is easier to write for someone else, your ideal reader. And you want that person to get what they need from the book, don't you? You want them to enjoy it, connect with it, love it, come back to it, review it, and tell others how great it was and how it changed them. Of course you do. Anyone who says otherwise might not be telling the whole truth. If you write only for yourself, I encourage you to think about your ideal readers and try writing for them instead. Try writing with the intention that your book will be for others, in service of others. Connect to this idea of service and you will write like you never have before.

HOW TO SERVE THE READER

Writing in service to your ideal reader is a powerful reframe. When you do this, you will find that you think differently about your content and how to approach your topic or story. In fact, there are three principles that will help you understand how to properly serve your reader. The first principle is that you must want to serve them and have a genuine desire to give them what they need and want. They have to matter to you, and you have to care. If you desire a successful book, look outside yourself and think about who you are writing it for. Who is this ideal reader?

Avoid simply coming up with a bunch of random facts and demographics. Instead, really think about this person and who they are. What is their life like? What do they struggle with? What are their fears, hopes, and dreams? What are they challenged by and what keeps them up at night?

Answer these questions first and foremost. Come up with a detailed understanding of who your ideal reader is and what their emotional experience is when buying your book. I encourage my authors to do this for fiction, nonfiction, memoir, and every type and genre of book. Make sure you are clear on who this person is, what drives them to your book, and how they feel when they come to the point of purchasing it.

If this exercise is tough for you and you feel stuck, I want you to go back to your *why* and think about why you have the desire to write this book about this topic to begin with. What's the driving force? What's your motivation? What my authors typically find is the book is being written for an earlier version of themselves. That is, they are writing the book they themselves needed five or ten years ago. That's really important to understand because as soon as you connect with this ideal reader who might have been similar to you five or ten years ago, you can tap into a way of writing that will feel more grounded, more authentic, more real, and much more in tune with what your ideal reader needs and wants. The important thing to understand is whatever you went through or experienced that brought you to the point of writing your book is needed not only by you but by others as well. Others may have had a similar experience, and your book could be the perfect fit for them. Do you see how this understanding of accountability will change the game forever?

Let's do an exercise. I want you to freewrite for five minutes about your book topic without stopping. The only thing you must focus on is writing for your ideal reader. Write *to* them, with them in mind. I would like you to do this exercise and then compare what you've written to some of your earlier writing about your book, perhaps another freewrite.

When you're finished, read what you've written and make the comparison. Do you see a tonal difference? Do you see any shifts in the language or the writing? Did it feel different while you were writing? If not, you're not quite there yet, and you need to dive deeper into who your ideal reader actually is.

Once you have a thorough picture of who your ideal reader is, the next thing you must dial in is their emotional experience when they come to the point of buying your book. The sooner you do this, the sooner everything will become clearer in your process and in your writing. This is because you can then understand what the end goal is for your reader and the number one outcome that they want. Do you see why that's valuable? Because you can help them accomplish that end goal through the contents of your book. This will allow you to focus and write with a single purpose. It will help you create a better book and become a better author.

Let's reflect on this for a moment. Think about the last time you purchased a book. Perhaps you went to browse your local bookstore and spent time looking at the latest bestsellers. Or maybe you were online and went to one of your online retailers to order a book you'd heard about. Maybe something caught your eye while you were shopping at the grocery store. Were you at the airport and looking for something to read during your flight? Think about this for a moment. Now the next question is what brought you to the point of buying this specific book. What emotions were you feeling at the time? What was the inner impulse to buy the book? Don't simply think about the circumstances or what you desired from the book. Think about the emotions you felt while buying it. Were you feeling intrigued and excited? Perhaps you were a little down in the dumps and wanted something inspirational. Or maybe you'd had a tough day at the office and felt determined to turn things around in your career. Perhaps one of your kids gave you a hard time about a new rule in the household and you felt irritated and in need of some parenting advice. Or maybe there was something eye-catching about the book that made you feel curious. Whatever it was, think back to that moment and write your emotions down on a piece of paper.

Finished? Good. What I want you to glean from this is that the reader is a human being with a very specific set of emotional experiences that will lead them to the point of buying your book. This is important because if you can get inside your reader's head and understand what their emotional experience will be when they come to the point of sale (POS) of your book, you can actually help to attract all the right readers and repel the ones that are not a fit for the book you are writing. Of course, we want as many readers as possible, but in truth, not everyone will be a good fit for your book. The point is to focus on who is a good fit so you can give them exactly what they need and want from your book and help them get the outcomes they desire. What are those outcomes and how do we deliver them? We'll dive into that in the next chapter as we continue to unpack how to create true accountability.

ACCESS THE CODE: IDEAL READER DEEP DIVE

I recorded a short video training on ideal readers and accountability mastery for authors that is a must-watch. To access it in the reader resources section of my website, visit **www.writingcoachla.com/thecode.**

VERONICA CAREY

I was terrified to start writing my book. One day, I was scrolling online and saw Ashley Mansour and her Book Accelerator® program. I scrolled past because my fear kept me from clicking on her page. But something nagged at me to go back, to click the button . . . and I've never looked back since.

Ashley's TAP Method was such a godsend. Having that structure offered me support and confidence and gave me hope! What a ride! The method offers eye-opening insight into what it realistically takes to write a book, and once I understood that reality, I knew I could write mine in even less than the 90 days touted. As such, I completed my book in just twenty-two days. As I write this, there's a huge smile on my face because I still cannot believe this outcome.

When my book was complete, I queried traditional publishers but ultimately decided to move into self-publishing due to the extremely long publication timelines given to me by the two publishing houses who made me offers. That's right—I had two offers! But my goal was to get the information in my book into the hands of as many high school and college students as I could as soon as possible. For this reason, going with Ashley's Bestseller Legacy program for publishing was a no-brainer.

The guidance and support I received from Ashley and her team was phenomenal. No question was a bad question, and everything was laid out in a manner that allowed me to reach short-term and long-term goals leading up to my launch day. My book launched to #1 bestseller status, and seeing the incredible outpouring of support in response was so amazing that I still cry just thinking about it. I honestly shed a wealth of tears during this writing-a-bestseller process in genuine celebration that I completed milestones I thought I would never achieve.

I am very proud of my book and all that has happened for me as a result of it. The US secretary of education sent me a hand-written accolade stating, "As a father and educator, the contents of this book are important to families and students." I also received special acknowledgment from my university, have appeared on over ten podcasts, and have been invited to be a guest lecturer at scores of presentations. I have also been paid to appear at speaking engagements across the country and have traveled abroad with my book to sell copies in the UK, India, and Pakistan. My book's website has attracted thousands of student visitors since its launch, and seeing my book on shelves in physical bookstores and my audiobook available on Spotify is like a dream. But best of all is witnessing how proud my parents are of my accomplishment—they can't stop sharing my book with all their friends!

I always say to anyone who is thinking about writing and publishing their own book: "Get yourself some Ashley!"

—VERONICA CAREY, assistant dean, associate clinical professor, and bestselling author of *Frame Your Degree*

CHAPTER NINE

BRAC Framework

A Recipe for Happy Readers

NOW THAT YOU KNOW who your ideal reader is and what their emotional experience is when they come to the point of buying your book, the next step to properly serving them is to think about what outcome the reader is hoping to achieve or receive by the end of the book. As the famous Russian writer Vladimir Nabokov once wrote, "Readers are not sheep, and not every pen tempts them."[13]

So how do we figure out what does tempt our readers and deliver what they want in our books? We use the BRAC framework.

BRAC stands for four words: *believe, receive, achieve,* and *conceive.* All readers, regardless of the genre they pick up, are looking for outcomes in these four areas. They may be reading because they hope the book will help them achieve some specific goal or will give them something specific and they will receive something from the reading experience. Or they may be reading in order to form new beliefs or enhance their existing beliefs around the subject matter or topic. Or lastly, they may be reading to conceive of a new thought, idea, or possibility. Often, your ideal reader will be reading for some combination of all these elements and looking to achieve, receive, believe, and conceive something new from the reading experience. It's up to you to understand what they desire in each of those four categories and provide those outcomes to them.

Imagine your book is that solution for the reader out there who most needs it. Imagine how it would feel knowing that every single day your book, your story, your message, your knowledge, is helping someone—many someones—out there feel more connected, less lonely, more understood, and happier.

This is why it's so important to lock in your ideal reader and the idea of truly serving them through your book utilizing the BRAC framework. Regardless of what you might think, your book isn't about you. It's about your reader and serving them exactly as they are hoping to be served. Remember, every single reader will come to your book with two things: 1) a clear emotional experience and 2) something they want to achieve, receive, believe, or conceive from reading.

When you know this, the writing becomes so much easier, and you can form true accountability in your writing habit now and forevermore.

YOUR BIG IDEA

Now that you understand how to develop true accountability and create happy readers, the next step is to put this into practice. To do that, we need to home in on your big idea. The big idea is something few aspiring authors think about clearly. They have an idea for a book, and they assume that's the book that should be written. But it's important to think about how your idea will be received by your ideal reader and make sure you are really writing the right book.

If you're tracking with me so far, we have covered:

- Why you are writing the book
- Who you are writing for and how to serve your ideal reader

Next, we are going to tackle the *what* in the equation—that is, what you are writing about. I will teach you a simple process to validate and lock in your big idea.

PART I: CLARIFY YOUR BIG IDEA

The first part of this exercise is to clarify your big idea. You may think you have clarity, but this is the time to go a layer deeper to really understand what you are writing and who you are writing for.

The first question to answer is what is your book's topic/subject or central premise? See if you can create a sentence that powerfully describes the topic or central premise. Do this even (and especially) if you are writing fiction.

Now, pause a moment and consider this question: why do you want to write about this? What moves you about it? What inspires you? What is the *why* lurking below the surface? What is the true driver of your aspirations? If you desire to write a book and grow your business to make over six figures annually, for example, that might appear to be your motivation—write a book that will grow your business. But beneath that, there's more driving you. Perhaps it's having the freedom to work fewer hours and spend more time with your family. Or maybe it is to fulfill a goal of being location-independent and traveling the world to experience new cultures. Whatever it might be, I urge you to discover the real driver and motiving factor for you. Take a few minutes to do this exercise right now, then fill in the blank below or write it in your notebook.

My deepest *why* is _____

As I have seen with my author students, their book topic usually connects to their deepest *why* in some way. This is especially true for their first books. It is maybe less true if you're writing your ninth book, but even then, you will find the initial impetus to write that ninth book comes from deep within. I have a theory that it's this very connection that makes the first book so difficult, in that it's connected to the self and requires deep, specific self-inquiry, but I'll save that for another conversation.

For now, we are going to keep breaking this down until your big idea is crystal clear. Next up, ask yourself, what are the main ideas that interest you about this project? List as many as you can, including any intermingled ideas that seem related. Put them all down so you have all the main ideas in one place.

Now, let's get more particular. Of all the main ideas listed above, find your top three. Limit yourself to three and only three. This may be difficult, but it's important. When you have done this, rank them in order.

1. _____

2. _____

3. _____

Of the top three ideas above, which do you feel most drawn to as a writer? Is it different from your initial premise or the same? Take a deeper look here and see what has emerged for you. The goal is once again to get really clear and specific about your book topic. Let me give you some examples of how this exercise has influenced aspiring authors and helped them to get clear on their books' big ideas.

I had a therapist writing a book about relationships and repairing marriages. Her topic wasn't defined beyond that until this exercise, when she realized she was really writing about a new way for couples to have healthy and effective communication. See the nuance? It's a different, more focused book.

A parenting coach thought he was writing a how-to book to help parents control their household and properly discipline their kids. What he realized after completing this exercise was that his desire was actually to write a book about understanding your kids better so that you connect with them, form a deeper relationship, and create a more peaceful living situation.

A fantasy author thought she was writing about a fictional world she had created, but when she did this exercise, she realized the big idea was about learning to accept yourself and own who you are, even when the world sees you as different.

I had a young writer who began writing a how-to book for new moms and soon realized her words were a soul-searching battle cry for young Latina women everywhere who wanted more out of life but weren't sure how to find it.

Powerful stuff, isn't it?

This is why the TAP Method is so helpful, because we prioritize answering these important questions at the beginning of our writing journey, rather than bumbling through and hoping we stumble upon the answers in a long-winded writing process. If you like efficiency, planning, and the ability to control your own destiny, the TAP Method is going to work well for you, and you will enjoy the process much more. What would you rather do, write aimlessly and hope you figure out your big idea and deepest *why* somewhere in the first draft, or use the TAP Method, do a few short exercises, and discover it before you ever put pen to paper?

I've done it both ways, and I know which way I'd rather write!

Writing with the TAP Method not only helped me write with more clarity and confidence, but it produced a better book in a shorter period of time. On top of that, it's how I've been able to become a # 1 Amazon and international bestselling author relatively quickly in my career. It can do the same for you too.

Dialing in your big idea helps you find the rawest, freshest, most intrinsically important idea that will drive your book and guide you in the writing process. As you go through this exercise and others, you may need to be open to asking yourself, *Is this really what I'm writing about?* Then, dig a layer deeper to see if there is more beneath the surface of your initial idea that you thought made up the topic for your book. When you do this exercise, your answers may surprise you.

This is the kind of work we do with our author students at the start of the 90-day Book Accelerator® writing program. We spend time discussing and looking deeply at what they want to write. They also do this introspective work independently or with one of our program coaches. The goal is the same, and you can do this for yourself now. Dig a layer deeper to see if there is anything you are missing, anything that needs to be considered or brought back that you've overlooked. Once you've done that work, ask yourself, *if you had to choose a single idea from the top three you wrote down, which would it be?* Describe why this idea is important to you and why you chose it after all this digging. You'll want to go back to the deepest *why* you wrote about earlier and see how it marries with your big idea. Do the two correlate? Can you find a connection between your deepest *why* and your big idea? You should see that they are connected, because from a powerful, deep *why* will often come a big idea of great clarity, specificity, and importance for the author.

Now that you have greater clarity on your big idea, you're going to spend a moment validating it for yourself. This is a quick assessment to gauge how you feel about the idea and where you may still have some gaps.

PART II: VALIDATE YOUR BIG IDEA

Complete the Big Idea Questionnaire below to see how your big idea stacks up. Remember, this isn't a quiz to see how good your big idea is or whether it's clear enough. This is all about your connection to the book topic and how you are feeling in preparation for your writing process. Why is this important? Because many aspiring authors have brilliant ideas for books but very little connection to the topic or subject matter.

Here's a quick example. One of my author students wanted to write two books: a memoir about her life and upbringing and a leadership book about her time serving overseas. Everyone had been telling her for years to write the leadership book, but it didn't excite her. Even though she thought it could be an interesting book for others to read, she didn't want to write it. The book that was really calling to her was her memoir, with the personal and professional stories of her life woven in. The leadership element would therefore make an appearance, but it wouldn't be the big idea. See the difference?

BIG IDEA QUESTIONNAIRE

Now, take the assessment below to validate your big idea and see how you score. Give yourself a ranking between one and ten, with ten being the highest, for the questions below. Then take your total score and multiply it by two to get a percentage out of one hundred. This is a spot check to see how strong your big idea is and how *you* feel about writing about it.

1. Rank how excited you are by your big idea as the focus of your writing project.
2. Rank how confident you are in your idea as the focus of your writing project.
3. Rank how much clarity you have around your idea as the focus of your writing project.
4. Rank how strongly you feel you can commit to your idea as the focus of your writing project.
5. Rank how strongly you feel about sharing this idea with potential readers and collaborators (editors, etc.) as the focus of your writing project.

Total Score x 2 = _____ out of 100%

How did you do? Let's analyze your score together.

If your total score is less than 85 percent, you will want to go back through the Big Idea Questionnaire and start again. Perhaps there is something else you should be writing about that wants to come out, or maybe you need to really consider your answers to each question to see what is lacking.

For example, I had an author student score below 85 percent because her answer to question one was really low. She had zero confidence in herself! When we talked about it, she really loved her big idea, but she still doubted herself and whether she could write that book. She felt like she wasn't qualified, so I had her do a little freewrite exercise on her deepest *why* once more and read it back. What she found was that she needed to shift her mindset and start believing in herself as a writer. All her life, she had been told to get a real job and ignore her impulse to write. Her family didn't value the stories about her life she'd written, so when it came to writing this bigger work that was based on her professional work as a therapist of over thirty years, she was stumped. It took time, but soon she realized her big idea was strong enough and she was the only person who could write this valuable book.

When you evaluate and validate your idea for yourself, understand that if you score really low—less than 85 percent—you either need another idea or you need to clarify something about the idea you currently have. Ask yourself what is holding you back and where your weak points are with this idea, then see if you can make it stronger. If not, it might be that you need to choose something else to write about.

Got your big idea in place? Good. The next step is to take all of this and move on to the *P* in the TAP Method, which stands for process. Writing and publishing a book successfully doesn't have to be mysterious. It all comes down to knowing the process. Trust me when I say that when you can see the path to write and publish your book, it becomes so much easier to walk it. That's why in the next chapter, we'll walk step by step through the writing and publishing process, and I'll show you how to master it for yourself.

Author Success Story
ANDY WAY

Since publishing my book through Ashley's Bestseller Legacy program, my exposure for my business has gone through the roof. I have been presented with so many incredible opportunities, and my overall credibility has soared to heights that seem to only come with the notoriety of being a successful published author.

I held an incredible book launch celebration hosted by a local luxury lifestyle company who then partnered with me for the month to help raise money for my favorite charity. From there, I earned an interview slot with a local TV station about my book and business, which led to being approached and hired to give a private talk at a Fortune 300 company!

Since then, I have been interviewed on dozens of podcasts, both in the US and abroad, and have joined the board of directors for the National Speakers Association in St. Louis. I've also accepted a position with a large nonprofit organization and spoken at events for their program graduates. I have been featured in two editions of a large, reputable local magazine and was asked by a TV personality with a thirty-year career to be interviewed on her new show. I'm now in talks to join her as a semipermanent cohost and travel and speak across the country.

My business and its related platforms have also grown exponentially since publishing my book. I turned it into a signature program with multiple offerings, including roundtables with a revenue projection of $60,000 to $80,000 each. I partnered with the Institute for Experiential Learning to deliver co-branded assessment and measurement tools and am working with them to develop a certification program. This will take my brand and business nationwide so we can scale for greater impact. I also created partnerships with two corporate off-site management companies in the US and UK to deliver my program to their clients.

But the very best part of it all? I feel confident and proud of the accomplishment and the work I'm doing to inspire and empower others with the tools needed to adjust to change, overcome challenges, and feel more alive.

Here's to living adventurously!

—ANDY WAY, bestselling author of *Always Adventure*

BECOME A MASTER OF PROCESS

CHAPTER TEN

The 6th Secret

Become a Master of Process

I MAGINE FOR A MOMENT having your book done, printed, and launched into the world in about a year or less. How would that feel? How would your family, colleagues, and friends react knowing you went from aspiring author to published, successful author in a handful of months? It can and does happen all the time! Writing and publishing a book need not take years of your life.

Yet so much of what goes into making a book is the details that happen behind closed doors, details most of us never realize even happen. This is part of the magic of making books, but it shouldn't be kept hidden from aspiring authors. Not if they want to understand how to write and create an amazing, life-changing book. Why? Because you must be able to see the pathway to publication so you can take the first step. You also need to be able to walk the entire pathway confidently, easily, and quickly.

The truth is, if you know the seven steps to writing and publishing a book, you can become a master of the process and do this for yourself! Of course, I always recommend that first-time authors seek out the support of a coach, mentor, or expert who can guide them through every step to avoid common pitfalls and make the process that much easier, faster, and more fun. If you don't have a coach or mentor yet, that's okay! I will guide you through the steps, pitfalls, and key linchpins of success in this chapter.

KNOWING THE PROCESS IS HALF THE BATTLE

When it comes to writing and publishing a book, knowing the process really is half the battle. How does the raw, unedited manuscript on your computer become the beautiful, polished, printed book on your shelf? That's the magical process that most first-time authors usually don't understand. Because of this, many jump the gun and start interviewing and pitching publishers before they've even written their books or properly planned them, which can lead to overwhelm and confusion and cause many aspiring authors to give up on their books early on. Editing also causes much confusion, since most first-time authors don't know when to hire an editor, what type of editor to hire, and what types of editing are best according to where they are in the process. To sum it up, many first-time authors have an oversimplified version of the process in their minds that looks something like this:

WRITE!  PUBLISH!

Needless to say, there are a lot of details missing!

The details we can't see make up a huge part of the writing and publishing processes for new authors. The goal of this chapter is to make the invisible steps of the book writing and publishing process visible for you because in order to become a master of process (the *P* in the TAP Method), you must first understand what the actual step-by-step process entails.

If you are not sure what publishing a book might entail, don't worry. It's not uncommon to not understand everything that goes into writing and publishing a book. That's typically why people have concerns about self-publishing and seek out publishers and publishing services instead, like my company's full-service, done-for-you self-publishing program, Bestseller Legacy, for example. It's also why when people begin the process of publishing a book they find there is a learning curve simply because they were not expecting many of the various steps that are a natural part of the path.

Unless you study book publishing in school or get a publishing degree, the ins and outs of book publishing are simply not common knowledge. When all we can see is the finished product sitting on our shelves, it's easy to misunderstand what goes into creating it. But like anything, a path you can see is much easier to walk than one you can't. Let's illuminate the path to publishing—the process of getting that book in print—so you can remove any fear or hesitation and take the first step!

THE UNPUBLISHED BOOK

There is nothing more unfortunate to a book lover than a book that holds a world of value sitting on the shelf somewhere, tucked away where no one can read it. Sadly, I have encountered many people with unpublished manuscripts sitting on their hard drives or in a drawer somewhere simply because they can't see the path to publishing. One such author I knew, whom we will call Rhonda, had written an amazing book on life lessons for young women. After completing the book, Rhonda began the journey into publishing but soon found herself overwhelmed by the process and the amount of information out there. Rhonda became frustrated by her lack of knowledge and not knowing what next step to take was best, and she soon shelved the book she had worked so hard to create. She later shared with me that after working with an outside editor (not one of our editors, who know and understand our specific process), she became even more daunted, froze, and simply put the book aside. More importantly, her dreams of writing and publishing had dwindled, all because she couldn't see the path to publishing clearly. And because of that, her book never reached a single reader.

You must be able to clearly see the path to publishing and have a direct step-by-step plan for how to get there. This is why it's my mission to make publishing extremely fast and easy and to produce high-quality books that rival traditionally published books through my full-service self-publishing program Bestseller Legacy.

As you read on, I want you to remember Rhonda's story of her shelved book and keep this in mind: not all editors are good editors. Not all book coaches are good book coaches. Not all publishers are good publishers. Just because someone purports to have industry knowledge and experience doesn't mean they actually have your best interest in mind or are qualified to guide you in the right way to reach your goals. There are many disgruntled and unhappy people working in the book business who have failed as authors in their own right. Many sit on the sidelines waiting for someone to come along who they can "help" only to discourage them from doing what they themselves could never accomplish. There are also many people who set up shop as publishers, editors, and coaches without the appropriate credentials and claim to have the knowledge and experience to help aspiring authors when in fact they do not.

Therefore, let's set a rule before we go deeper: do not listen to anyone who isn't qualified or who has a negative or embittered view of the world of books and publishing. In fact, be wary of listening to anyone who has a negative and embittered view of the world, period! Use your critical mind to think it through, look at their credentials, and realize that what they say is not necessarily fact or truth but a subjective opinion. And as you will see and begin to embody from the teachings I share in this book, what you think and choose to believe matters greatly in terms of accomplishing your dreams of writing and publishing a book, or many books, in your lifetime.

Your thoughts and beliefs are a very significant part of the equation, so beware anyone who lacks experience or has the kind of negative, discouraging, unsupportive, poor mindset that is going to discourage you from your goals and dreams. You cannot, I repeat, *cannot* afford to have your mindset and thinking compromised by those embittered by their own lack of accomplishment in the same field. We will return to this point later, but for now, as we embark on the journey together and I illuminate the path to publishing for you, remember my rule and protect your mindset at all costs.

THE JOURNEY TO BECOMING AN AUTHOR: THE STAIRCASE

To walk the path to publishing, you need to be able to see it clearly. I think of the path to publishing as a staircase of many steps, each one specific and clear, moving you closer to your goal of a finished, published, bestselling book that creates the impact you desire.

The path to publishing a bestselling book looks like this:

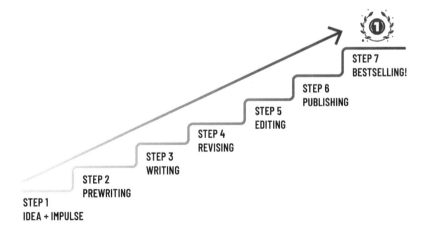

As a book coach and publishing service provider, my entire line of work is to make the process from the first step to the last easier, faster, and smoother for my authors. In this chapter, we'll cover what the seven steps entail, then in the next chapter, I will show you the key linchpins of success that help our authors progress through all seven steps to a bestselling book in a fraction of the time it normally takes first-time authors. While it can take years to do this, my goal is for you to go from your raw idea to a published bestseller in one year or less. That is the transformation we create for our authors and the one I desire for you too. But the transformation requires that the author take the first step in that journey and not quit along the way.

So, what is that journey to getting your book published? Let's walk that path together.

STEP ONE: IDEA AND IMPULSE

Step one, the idea and impulse stage, is where most people are in the process of writing and publishing. I call it the idea and impulse stage because you most likely have an idea (or many ideas) of what you want to write about and the impulse to write a book. The definition of *impulse*, according to Merriam-Webster, is "a sudden spontaneous inclination or incitement to some usually unpremeditated action."[14] If you have the impulse but no idea, or the idea without the impulse, that usually leads to inaction. When you have an idea *and* the impulse to write about that idea, that's how you know you're on step one of the staircase. We'll talk in a moment about how you move from each step to the next, but for now, let's get clear on the overall journey.

STEP TWO: PREWRITING

Prewriting is the step of the process that includes all the research, planning, preparation, and foundational writing you do before you write the actual manuscript, or the first draft of the book itself. It's an important step that often gets missed by first-time authors, who jump the gun and start writing without this crucial step. This leads them to get stuck and stop writing because the essential work they should have done to prepare themselves to write the first draft never happened. It's like trying to run a marathon without ever training for it. Prewriting isn't only foundational, it is essential. And as I'll show you later, making an outline in the prewriting phase is only part of the equation. Remember, the prewriting needed before the writing starts will bring the results you crave: a well-written, completed book that you can be proud of.

STEP THREE: WRITING

Step three of the process, the writing phase, is where most people start. It's also where most people stop. Most people do not get past trying to write the first draft. They start out gung ho and excited, inspired by a dream or some flash of inspiration. They take that to the page, write for two or three days, sometimes a few weeks or months, and then quit. They run out of steam, and with the inspiration gone and their original *why* elusive and evading them, they simply give up and stop writing, unsure of how to return to the book or what to do with what they have written. This is precisely the experience we don't want, but it's the most common experience new writers have in the book writing and publishing process, especially if they skip prewriting. I'll share more about this in the next chapter. For now, let's continue on the pathway to publishing so you can master the process, the *P* in the TAP Method.

STEP FOUR: REVISING

Step four in the writing and publishing process is revising. Revising is where the author reviews their manuscript and begins to rework the material as necessary. Typically, the few who get to this phase do so out of sheer willpower and then find the revision phase painstaking and exhausting because they don't know how to revise correctly. Additionally, because so many people skip prewriting, they end up with a messy, unviable manuscript that they need to rewrite altogether. That's why revision can feel so hard for new authors and is another place in the process where many people give up, if they haven't before getting here. Again, this is why with the TAP Method in my Book Accelerator® program, we emphasize prewriting early on, so the books my author students write end up cleaner, more organized, and needing far less revision at this stage. Later, I will share with you some handy revision tips we teach our author students to help them make revision faster and easier.

STEP FIVE: EDITING

Step five, editing, is when an outside editor helps the author develop and polish the book prior to publication. There are many different types of editors and editing. Therefore, it's really important to know who the right fit for your book at this crucial stage is. I've seen more than my fair share of bad editors who, as in the case of Rhonda with her women's advice book, can make or break your career. A good editor is a gift to the author, to the book, and to the readers who will receive it. A bad editor is a blight from which the author often never recovers.

How does one spot the difference? The truth is that many novice writers don't. They trust in unqualified and inexperienced editors. The best way to know you have the right editor? Get the editor to do a sample edit. Even then, it's very difficult for a first-time author to know what to look for in the sample, so my best advice is to hire an expert publishing consultant to assist you.

The last point about editing is that many people don't know the difference between an editor and a book coach, but it is substantial: editors work with you once there are words on the page (ideally all of them!), while book coaches help you formulate your ideas, build your confidence, and gain the clarity needed to get the words on the page in the first place. Book coaches—like me, for example—can be utilized from the very beginning of the process, before the first draft, whereas editors are best utilized only at the appropriate editorial stage and not before. While some editors are book coaches and some book coaches are editors, it's important to know the difference between these two roles so you get the right support for your book at the right time.

STEP SIX: PUBLISHING

Step six of the process is publishing, which includes all the activities necessary to get the book launched and available to readers. This includes marketing and promoting the book. It used to be that you had to know someone in publishing and have a big fancy publisher to get the book into your readers' hands. There was only really one option, which is known as traditional publishing. Today, however, there are more ways to publish a book than ever before. You have traditional publishing, but you also have hybrid or partner publishing and self-publishing. Note that I will not be covering vanity publishing (where an author pays a publisher and gives up many of their publication rights and royalties with little control) in this book because I don't believe it is in the best interest of authors. For now, know that there are three paths to publishing—traditional, hybrid or partner publishing, and self-publishing—and each one is its own distinct route.

The route you decide to take will influence many things, like whether you retain the rights to your book, whether you control things like the cover, and what kind of help you will have with all the final touches to create the physical paperback, hardback, and audiobook. It will also influence how much money you can earn from your book sales (your percentage of the royalties); whether it is sold online, in bookstores, or both; and lastly, whether you have a shot at becoming a bestselling author, something I believe everyone should attempt to accomplish.

A word here about marketing: many aspiring authors I've spoken with seem to have an aversion to marketing. If that is the case for you, I urge you to rethink your position on this and open your mind to learning marketing. Marketing is not only an essential part of authorship, but it is absolutely necessary for the book to be published successfully, regardless of which of the three publishing paths you choose. Many aspiring authors avoid self-publishing and seek out publishers because, as they tell me, they don't want to "worry about the marketing" and want someone to do that for them. The truth is most publishers, large or small, that you work with today will ask to see your marketing and promotion plan for your book. Regardless of how you publish, you will ultimately be responsible for marketing and promoting your book. Of course, there are people you can hire to help you with marketing or even do parts of the book marketing for you, as we do in our Bestseller Legacy publishing program, but the fact remains that marketing is always the author's responsibility, so I encourage you to embrace it and get help from experts who can make it simple and easy.

STEP SEVEN: BESTSELLING

Step seven in the process is your book becoming a bestseller once you've published it. Many people count themselves out of this phase altogether, and once they know they are to be published, they relinquish the book to the publisher and dissolve themselves of the thought of becoming a bestseller. This is a mistake. Every single author should be thinking about how to make their book a bestseller from the beginning of their writing and publishing journey. A bestseller campaign should be built into your launch strategy from day one. I encourage you not to settle for anything less than a bestseller because it's simple to achieve if you understand the process and something people value and appreciate. Being a bestseller means your book outsold the competition at a particular time. It also means you supported that result with your own marketing and advertising activities. This is something to be extremely proud of, and yet many first-time authors shy away and count themselves out of the bestseller race early in the process.

Bestselling status is a numbers game. Having the right number of sales in the right number of categories at the right time is virtually how every bestseller list works—except *The New York Times*. (That list is the gold standard, and it is based on more than raw numbers; it is actually editorially curated.) Amazon, *USA Today*, *Publishers Weekly*, and other bestseller lists, however, are similar in that they go by how many copies of a format of a book are sold in a given period of time and rank books based on this. Obviously, we could go deeper into the nuances of each list, but what I would like you to understand is that these lists are purely based on numbers. That's it! Understanding the numbers game is something we've mastered, and it's how we've helped all our authors in our Bestseller Legacy publishing program become bestselling authors on Amazon, Barnes & Noble, Kobo, and other platforms. You can do the same.

We will talk more about what is required for a bestseller in the next chapter, and I'll show you how simple it can be for you and your book.

So, there you have it. Seven steps of the staircase. Just seven steps of the book writing and publishing process, from idea and impulse in step one to publishing and bestselling in steps six and seven. The seven steps don't need to be hard, but the truth is most people make the process harder than it needs to be. My goal is to not only show you the seven steps but to take you by the hand and show you how to make the journey easier, faster, and more fun, as I do for my author students.

I've found the key to walking the entire staircase successfully starts with step one. When you know you are supposed to be an author, when you feel the impulse in your gut, when your idea won't leave you alone, when you can't seem to shake the nagging sense that you are meant for this, that's when you need to move beyond step one.

But how many people have the intense inner knowing I've described and actually make it beyond step one, the idea and impulse phase, into step two, the prewriting phase?

The answer? Very few.

Most people never move beyond step one, and this phenomenon is why I do the work that I do in the world. Because moving beyond step one is vital to your success as an author. I've spent a great deal of time trying to unpack and understand why it is that so many people have the idea and the impulse and yet never move beyond this phase, never take action to bring their books to life.

What is it that keeps so many aspiring writers stuck—trapped, even—at step one, the idea and impulse phase? What's missing from their equation, and how can we learn from this and fill in the gaps for you so that you can move forward and walk the entire staircase, step by step?

That is exactly the topic of the next chapter.

ACCESS THE CODE: YOUR PATH TO PUBLISHING

I filmed a quick video training for you about the writing and publishing process that goes deeper than this chapter and will help you figure out exactly how to get published. To access it in the reader resources section of my website, visit **www.writingcoachla.com/thecode.**

LYNN BROMLEY

When you write and publish a book, it makes you exponentially more credible—even if the people you're speaking to haven't read it yet. Being able to say that I'm a published author has been no small thing, doing wonders for my business and beyond.

I had wanted to write a book for decades, but like so many, I couldn't stick with any sort of schedule or outline that kept me going, so I pretty much gave up before I ever really started. But working with Ashley changed that. For one, I actually finished the book. Secondly, the process also changed my mindset about my words and my work being enough . . . ironically, a mindset I teach about in my book.

My book became an Amazon bestseller and has had a 4.9-star average rating since it came out. I have also been invited to appear on several podcasts thanks to my book's exposure and success. And after speaking about my book for an innovation conference in Iceland, I was offered a board position for an Icelandic startup company. But beyond all else, what this book has enabled me to do is become known for what my real passion is: gender equality.

Amazing things can happen if you take the leap and trust the process!

—LYNN BROMLEY, former Maine state senator, founder of Fintech Advocate consulting, and bestselling author of *On the Path to Justice*

I'm the type of person who sets a goal and sticks with it until I see it through. But even with the best of intentions and habits, actually completing writing your first book can be tough if you don't know what the best practices are for getting the task done, and done well. So I knew I didn't want to go it alone.

That made Ashley and her Book Accelerator® and Brands Through Books programs a no-brainer for me. I wrote my book in 90 days, then published it on Amazon 6 months later and became an overnight bestseller, with over 4,000 copies sold since publishing and counting. I might have been able to write and publish my book completely on my own, but it never would have been to the same level of expertise or success without Ashley and her team's help.

Thanks to that help, my book allowed me to build and launch my first online management course, expanding my business and reach exponentially. I have also been invited to speak about my book at large events in Hong Kong, London, Cambridge, New York, and Washington, DC. It has truly been the greatest boost for my executive coaching and strategic consulting business.

I highly recommend finding the right team to support you on this journey. Ashley and her experts are exactly the right team.

—TALBOT A. Stark, CEO and founder of ExecPathfinders, LLC
and bestselling author of *Elite Performance for Managers*

CHAPTER ELEVEN

KEY LINCHPINS OF SUCCESS

HOW DO WE WRITE a book we know will get published? To answer that, we need to understand the key linchpins of success for first-time authors between step one of the writing and publishing process (idea and impulse) and step seven (bestselling). As I covered in the last chapter, many people consistently misunderstand the writing and publishing process. On the surface, it seems simple enough, yet most people get it wrong. *Really* wrong. What do they do? They conflate and confuse the phases of the process. This means they don't follow the process linearly. Instead, they try to do more than one phase at a time.

For example, the number one challenge most aspiring authors have is that they attempt to edit their book while they are still writing it. It seems innocent enough, and many of us are taught to write this way in school. We are taught to create a single sentence and then go back and tweak, edit, and rework the sentence until it is a glowing example of the written word. The problem with this is that new writers are usually very bad editors, and they are even worse editors of their own work. To put it bluntly, the exercise of editing while writing is highly unproductive for people and wastes a lot of time and energy, as they switch gears from writing to editing and back again.

When you're writing the first draft, you are simply supposed to be a writer, not an editor. I teach my authors how to do this through a powerful writing technique called the Sandbox Method, based on a quote by author Shannon Hale: "When writing a first draft, I have to remind myself constantly that I'm only shoveling sand into a box so later I can build castles."[15]

If you have trouble with writing consistently without editing and you feel drawn to attempt both at once, you may want to determine if your work or career has made you extra cautious about writing that imperfect first draft and writing without going back and editing your work. I find that our author students who have built a career with words and correctness find this very hard. My English majors who work in journalism, advertising, copywriting, and the medical and technical fields in particular find this way of writing to be challenging, but the truth is it's more challenging to try to write your book and edit it at the same time, because when you edit while writing, you slow yourself down by conflating two activities that should actually be done separately.

So how exactly do we stop conflating and confusing the phases of the process to focus on one at a time? The first thing to understand is that there is only one job you must focus on at every stage of the process. We call these the key linchpins of success.

KEY LINCHPINS OF SUCCESS

I had an author student who was a coach who helped people overcome anxiety with her four-step method. The work she was doing in the world was the work she herself most needed, since she also struggled with anxiety. She had doubts about the process and whether she could get her book done. She had been thinking about it for years, and the idea was starting to weigh heavily on her heart. I knew the first critical step was for her to move out of the idea phase and into the prewriting phase.

The key to moving beyond step one is to decide and take action. It sounds so simple, yet you would be surprised how many aspiring authors lack the ability to do just that. They do not seem to have the capacity to make the decision that needs making. Most don't even realize this is required of them. Those who do decide, or think they have decided, don't take action. They freeze up, fight against their own decision, and convince themselves to go back on that which they have decided. Why is this?

The truth is neither I nor anyone else can make someone write a book. It must come from within. The power of the decision to write your book, therefore, is yours and yours alone. It is a power you can wield or not wield. The consequences of not deciding are that you will stay in the idea and impulse stage for the rest of your life and die with your book inside of you. Tragic and dark as that may sound, it's the truth.

Raymond Charles Barker wrote extensively about the power of decision in his book of that title. He talks about what it means to decide, how we begin to understand how we decide things for ourselves, and how our own decisions shape our thoughts, feelings, and experience of reality. What I know about aspiring authors—and anyone wishing to act on a creative impulse—is this: the decision must be made in the mind before it can be acted upon. It must be a clear and powerful thought (a decision) before it can be a clear and powerful action. Even when a solution—like my proven book writing system, the TAP Method, for example—is presented to these aspiring authors, they will not move forward and do anything until the decision has clearly been made in their minds and outwardly articulated.

So, back to the core question. Why do some aspiring authors decide to take the first step and others don't?

Many people never do this for one simple reason: they don't trust themselves to write the book, and fear and self-doubt win.

As we've discussed, many people fear not being successful with their books, that all the hard work and difficulty will be for naught. It's a legitimate fear, since many people who write their first draft do not actually go on to publish because they claim they don't have what it takes. This is almost never true. What *is* true is that they are fearful of putting themselves and their work out there. I get it! Writing and publishing a book can be scary. You open yourself up to other people's opinions, and some may not like what you've written. Yet the option that is far more frightening to me is to let your work and your experiences wither and die inside of you or on a hard drive somewhere. This is not the way! Your work deserves a place in the world, to be read, enjoyed, and appreciated! Your story and message deserve to be shared with others, but until you start believing it, you will continue to hold yourself back from making the ultimate decision and taking action.

This is why most aspiring authors remain on step one their entire lives and never take action, because of the fear and self-doubt gremlin. It's a horrible little monster that, if you allow it, will consume everything you allow it to, even your dreams of becoming an author. It will diminish your desire to be, to do, and to have more. There is no getting away from the fear and self-doubt gremlin when it gets this big except to do away with it. Yes, you really must kill it. Check your gremlin right now. Get acquainted with it. See what it's feeding on. No doubt it's there for a reason. It thinks it's protecting you and keeping you safe. I suppose, if you feel inclined, you can thank it for that. Or you can give the overprotective gremlin the boot and let it know that you got this, that your dreams are closer than you think, and that you are on a path to achieve them.

Once you have made this leap, it's time to decide and take action. It's not simply a nod of the head and a verbal "Yes, I am writing a book." So many people say this! In fact, ask any writing coach or editor you can find, and they will tell you they have heard this statement hundreds of times. But the tenacity and the commitment to finish a book is not the same thing as the flippant statement of saying you're writing one. Many people say it, but few really do it.

Why is this? For all the reasons this book has given you and more. But the reason I want to instill in you here and now is that when you say you're writing a book but don't follow through, it means you are lacking a powerful decision. You made a surface-level decision only, not one you have embodied fully in your being. In other words, you never internalized the decision and allowed it to become part of your identity. Noninternalized decisions are something we see all the time. It's become normal in our culture to say one thing and do another.

The word *decision* is very clear. Its Latin root, *decidere,* means to literally cut off. Cut off from what? Cut off from all else, all other possibilities. That means that when one makes a decision, there is no going back on that decision. To really decide is to cut yourself off from all other possibilities, to make a definitive decision that declares, "I'm doing this, and nothing is going to stop me." That's the essence of a true decision. The problem today is we've come up with a whole bunch of reasons, excuses, and circumstances that can keep us from our decisions. We decide, and then we take it back. We decide, but then something comes up. We decide, but then we change our mind. We decide, and then life happens.

Since I started this work, I've heard every tale you can imagine from those who aspire to have a book, long to have a book, and hope to have a book but have not and still cannot *decide* to have a book. Equally, I have heard every excuse under the sun for why someone cannot write their book. Why heaven and earth have been moved to prevent them from doing the one thing their soul, their heart, and their God call them to do. From sick animals, to the loss of loved ones, to moving house, to not enough time, to catastrophic events, and on and on and on, the truth is anything and everything will keep you from writing your book if you let it because you haven't decided. And yet, nothing can keep you from writing it once you do. That is the power of decision.

KEY LINCHPINS OF SUCCESS IN STEP TWO TO THREE: FROM PREWRITING TO WRITING

Getting from step two to three in the process, from prewriting to writing, requires another linchpin. Once you decide and take action, it's all about taking the right action. You don't want to waste your efforts doing things that don't work. And yet that is the mistake most aspiring authors make. They spin their wheels prewriting in a way that doesn't serve them. Most people start with an outline. Please don't do this! In my courses, the outline is actually the last step we do in prewriting. There are steps we do before this, before we build the final road map for the writing journey. The gap here is something I call the strategy gap, and it's what I am filling for you in this book, in my courses, and in my seminars.

I've never met an aspiring author with a good strategy. They simply don't know where to start and what to focus on first. To fill the strategy gap, you need a few things. You need the TAP Method (which you are learning right now,) but you also need to understand what goes into strategy, namely the three *P*s and the three *C*s. The three *P*s are *process*, *plan*, and *preparation*, and you should not begin writing until you have these three things. The first thing you need is a process. I am, in fact, breaking down the process here for you, but you also need to understand how to maximize your writing process. You should have a proven process to follow, and that is why the TAP Method (mastery of time, accountability, and process) is so valuable for day-to-day writing. You should know exactly what to focus on at any given time so you don't waste a moment and maximize your output with a very efficient input.

This is exactly what we do in Book Accelerator®, our 90-day book writing program that helps aspiring authors go from idea to finished draft in 90 days. We give you the proven writing process, as well as the *plan* and the correct *preparation* to follow step by step. By the end of the program, you have a finished book that you are ready to begin publishing! This means you have a complete first draft in 90 days, a draft that is ready for revision, editing, and then publishing! Exciting, right? It is to me because I've seen that 100 percent of the people who follow our process and complete the steps of our program not only finish amazing books but go on to become bestsellers and use their books to create amazing careers and thriving businesses. It is awesome!

The second part of filling the strategy gap is what I call the three *C*s: *confidence*, *clarity*, and *commitment*. Confidence is the internal belief that you can trust yourself to do a thing or figure out how to do a thing. A confident writer is more likely to become a committed writer. Why? Because they are willing to exercise courage more than those without confidence. Confidence isn't something you either have or don't have; it's something that can be built. As high-performance coach and author Brendon Burchard says, "Competence creates confidence."[16] So, for my author students to gain the confidence they need, they must simply develop greater competence in the skills required. What are those skills? We start with the basics and get them to master their mindset, then time, accountability, and the process with the TAP Method. After that, I start talking about the craft and get them thinking about the way they write as opposed to the method with which they write, as the two things are very different.

Clarity is the second skill. We use clarity to help author students find their way and get really clear on what it is they are writing, who it's for, the path to get the book where it needs to go, and what will happen next for them. The more light I can shed on the process, the better. Clarity isn't only about seeing clearly, however. Clarity is about deepening one's awareness altogether. Recently, I was speaking to one of my author students who had experienced this for herself. "The big aha came for me with the pro-outline," she said. "I have written books before, but not like this. There was a moment when I saw it—the whole book. And I knew that this was the way. This was the way I would write this book and every single book in the future." Needless to say, this particular author went on to publish, become a bestseller, and be very successful. I have no doubt she will become a voice in her field that stands out and changes the world.

You must have the three *P*s and the three *C*s to start your book and finish it. You must have them to publish it too. And guess what? You will need them again in the marketing effort and in your bestseller launch campaign. You'll also need them when you leverage the book into profitable channels. But most people don't have the three *P*s or the three *C*s in their writing strategy. Heck, most people don't have any strategy at all!

This is a good time to check in with yourself and ask: "Do I have the three Ps and the three Cs?"

If you don't, that's okay! It's why you're reading this book. It's the first step to putting a solid plan in place for your book. And by the end of reading this book, it's my hope that you can look back and realize you have gained all three.

Let's imagine for a moment that you have the three Ps and three Cs in place and that you follow a proven path like we do in Book Accelerator®, our 90-day book writing program. In a few weeks, your manuscript is done. You celebrate. You are ecstatic with joy and relief! But then a new question comes to mind because you know you are not done yet: "What do I do next?" What are the necessary steps from here to get the book published? Let's walk the rest of the path together in the next chapter.

ACCESS THE CODE: POWERFUL PLANNING PROMPTS

Need help with your three Ps and three Cs? I've got an additional freewriting resource for you with powerful prompts to help you fill in the gaps with the three Ps and three Cs! To access it in the reader resources section of my website, visit
www.writingcoachla.com/thecode.

LOUISE SEIRMARCO-YALE

I wrote my book to make an impact on those willing to look at art and its place in their daily lives, not for the profit of selling a book. But I still wanted to become a bestselling author so that my message could reach as many people as possible. Now I am one because of Ashley Mansour.

I meet many "wannabe" authors who have years-old manuscripts just sitting in a drawer somewhere. That's a great start, but having a book idea and writing some things down about it is far different from knowing how to successfully publish it. You have to be willing to admit that and seek the right support to achieve it.

The publishing world was an ocean of mystery for me. As an eighty-something-year-old, I have learned not to ask how to do something, but rather who I know who has already done it successfully. The answer to that was Ashley. She and her team at Brands Through Books gave me an arsenal of proven strategies that I would never have found on my own. They took the lead, I followed, and voila! Done! Published in record time and to that coveted bestseller status I'd always wanted.

If I had not chosen Ashley, with her fail-safe methods and generous spirit, I don't know where I'd be now. Many coaches hold back crucial information to retain superiority, but I know without a doubt that Ashley gave me everything, plus the encouragement to carry through with it. She gave me confidence that my book was a winner! And it is. I am very grateful I chose her, a true expert.

Thanks to the exposure from my book, I now write an art column for my local newspaper. My book has generated interest from a renowned arts magazine in a feature article about me. I held a retrospective art show which generated sales and publicity.

I am constantly invited to events as a speaker, sponsor, and book signer. Businesses are interested in showcasing my work, which is great exposure. I now have a YouTube channel about my work. People really and truly do pay attention to me differently now because of my book.

Artists are a dime a dozen, but a published author and woman artist is unique. I am introduced differently now. The book immediately signals authority to my audiences, that I am a "real" artist and so much more. Thank you, Ashley and team. You are not just my guiding light but my friends.

—Louise Seirmarco-Yale, bestselling author
of *Art, You Be the Judge*

CHAPTER TWELVE

THE STEPS TO GETTING PUBLISHED

R EMEMBER RHONDA, who shelved her book and never got it published? What I'm about to teach you will help ensure that your book doesn't also end up shelved and collecting dust. When you follow the easy steps I've set out for you, that won't happen. That's why this section of the book is all about getting your manuscript made into the physical book you see on the shelves.

The first step to do that is to take your raw, unedited first draft and put it through the process of revision. You must make the book better. Notice that I didn't say you must make the book *perfect*. You do not have to make it perfect. It only has to be better than it was initially. A lot of writers feel uncertain at this phase. They worry about what revision will take and how they will make the book better. As a consequence, many wind up in what I call the revision graveyard, where books go to die. I know it sounds dramatic, but I've seen it happen when first-time authors end up rewriting and revising the book many times, often with the assistance of one or more editors, and they never finish! This typically happens when they write the book without a strategy like the TAP Method to keep them grounded and adhering to their process.

How do you prevent yourself from falling into this trap and keep moving along the path to publishing, bestselling, and creating everything you desire? You simply must have the key linchpin in place, which is appropriate guiding feedback. Guiding feedback is a special kind of feedback that is not at all like the red marks on paper that your English teacher gave you. It's the kind of feedback that slowly guides you, nurtures you, and supports you along the way to reach your end goal. Sadly, most authors don't know how to get this feedback because most editors and coaches don't know how to give it in the first place! This creates something I call the feedback gap.

Filling the feedback gap requires two things that are absolutely necessary for any writer to begin revisions in an appropriate way, a way that allows them to avoid the revising and editing black hole. Those two things are

1. Distance and perspective
2. Quality feedback and encouragement

Let's discuss both of these so we can fill in the feedback gap together.

DISTANCE AND PERSPECTIVE

Distance allows the author to see what they need to see and separate themselves emotionally, psychologically, and intellectually—sometimes even spiritually—from their work. They need to stop being so close to it. To do that, they need to step away from it for a period of time to increase their distance to the work and gain perspective.

Perspective is all about shifting your point of view to be able to see what you couldn't see before. Imagine being at the base of a mountain. You can see the horizon, but the trees block everything around you. To gain perspective—a full 360-degree view of everything—you need to climb the mountain and get distance from where you once stood, thus gaining a greater perspective of what is around you. Explorers would often do this when they were trying to find new territories to scout and needed to understand the landscape. It gives one a bird's-eye view of things, a holistic impression of all that is around them. This is exactly what we want to do with our books. It is absolutely essential that you not only gain perspective but distance yourself from the work so that it no longer feels like it's yours. Of course, logically you know it is yours, but you really want to be far enough removed that you ask yourself, "Did I really write this?" Not in a critical way, but more in an observant, objective way.

This is the greatest vantage point from which to begin revisions because you have distance from and a perspective of the entire work and can form a true opinion of it. Forming a true opinion of your work is an important factor that usually gets overlooked. Every successful author I know relies on editors and beta readers to report on what they think of the book. But they themselves also take the time to do these steps to figure out what they think of their own work. When you do, it will be very easy to revise and make your book better because you will be able to clearly see what it needs.

QUALITY, OBJECTIVE FEEDBACK AND ENCOURAGEMENT

To fill the feedback gap, you need to gather quality, objective feedback. The reason many first-time authors have a difficult time getting this kind of feedback is because many editors are a) unqualified or b) qualified technically but lacking in the tact and nuance required to deliver feedback to first-time authors in an appropriate manner. They simply plunk their comments down, make their corrections, and expect that the author will be able to take it from there. But more often than not, the first-time author freezes up when they get the edits and goes into analysis paralysis, not knowing what to do next. This is because the first-time author has a unique set of needs, since the experience of editing and being critiqued is so entirely new to them.

When looking for an editor for your book, you want someone who can guide you with a firm but gentle hand, is qualified, and has edited books in your genre before that have gone on to be published and, ideally, become bestsellers. You also want someone who understands your goals and will support you in your choice of how to publish your book. You want someone who has a genuine interest in the work as well so they can edit the book in an insightful and engaged manner. Lastly, you want someone who can provide objective feedback in a way that is skillful and mindful of your own inclinations and ability to receive the feedback.

If you are a first-time author, you will want to find an editor who can provide you with exceptional encouragement. Believe me when I say you want your editor to be a good cheerleader, someone who will let you know what is working and what you're doing well and champion that. Then you want them to adequately help you in the areas that need work. Having your book edited and critiqued can feel challenging, and while you do need the right mindset and thick skin to handle that critique, it also really helps if your editor knows how to cheer you on and recognize the positive aspects of your work as well.

It's that simple, and yet also that difficult, because editors are trained to be critical. They are taught to be highly detail-oriented and to pick out the smallest thing—the placement of a comma, the em dash instead of the en dash, the usage of a single word over another. They are trained to notice what's wrong with a book so that it can be fixed. Sometimes, out of their training, a rather harsh and overly critical, analytical demeanor can emerge in the editor over time. If you find an editor like this, they may not be the right person for you to work with at first. Find an editor who knows how to balance good editing and quality feedback with giving support, encouragement, and helpful guidance. Remember, this advice is for the first-time author. If you are a seasoned author, you may have moved past the stage of needing the positive reinforcement that new authors require. From my experience, however, positive reinforcement works wonders for everyone!

Now it's time for a little positive reinforcement right here. As we dive into the next section, I would like you to take a deep breath and know that wherever you are in your journey, all things are possible and you *can* do this! Whatever doubt or uncertainty may still linger within you will be eradicated as we move through the next few chapters of this book. Keep reading, because the secrets I have in store for you will really boost your confidence and further light the path toward becoming the successful author you desire to be!

NOT ALL EDITS ARE CREATED EQUAL

It's important to know that there are multiple types of editing and not all editing is the same, nor is it all done at once. It is a process, like anything! Having the right editor by your side during each phase of the editorial process is crucial. Having the right support from revision to editing and beyond will make all the difference as you near publishing and ready the book for others to receive. Below are the basics to help you understand what types of editing are available to you and when you should make use of them.

DEVELOPMENTAL EDITING

Also called substantive editing, big-picture editing, content editing, or structural editing, developmental editing looks holistically at the entire book for things like structure, tone, voice, plot, character, argument, a through line, and more. Different developmental editors will focus on different things. Some may do light copy editing throughout the book, while others will focus primarily on the big-picture elements of the book.

It's important to note that many publishers and publishing services skip this editorial step because it is the most expensive type of editing. It is also the most essential, which is why we recommend all our authors who publish with us in our Bestseller Legacy publishing program have a developmental editor.

The best time to have your manuscript developmentally edited is after you have finished your first draft and made any revisions that you can see need to be made. When you can't see what else to fix or how to make the book better, that's the time to hire a developmental editor. Be careful here, though, because theoretically, you could always see something to fix with your own work.

LINE EDITING

This type of editing is performed by a line editor who works line by line to improve the flow, meaning, and style of the writing. Line editors are a wonderful resource for first-time authors because, unlike copy editors, they are concerned with the stylistic changes that make the book better, whereas copy editors are primarily concerned with the mechanics of writing. Line editing isn't necessary for every book, however. But if you do decide to have this type of edit done, it should only occur after your developmental edit is complete.

COPY EDITING

A copy edit involves looking at the mechanics of each sentence, primarily for correctness. Details that copy editors look for include things like correct spelling, grammar, diction, syntax, and the placement of citations. They may also look at the consistency of the work from one section to the next.

All manuscripts need copy editing, which should only be performed after line editing is complete. If a line edit is determined to not be needed for a manuscript, then copy editing should occur after the developmental edit is complete.

PROOFREADING

Whereas copy editing looks for correctness, proofreading looks for errors. In this type of editing, the concern of the editor is whether there is an error in the text. They are scanning to ensure the text is error-free rather than reading for meaning, context, or style. At this final stage of the editing process, the manuscript should be very clean with few errors. Multiple proofreads may be required to achieve this, or the proofreader may encourage the author to complete a thorough copy edit if the manuscript still has too many errors to warrant a proofread.

A WORD ABOUT BETA READERS

You may have heard the term *beta readers* before. Beta readers can be a helpful part of the writing and publishing process for various reasons. Some authors like to have beta readers to spot-check their content, get an idea of how their ideal readers would respond, or even help them ensure the subject matter is up to snuff. With fiction, they are commonly used to get an idea of the quality of the book, including plot, conflict, characters, and world-building. In nonfiction, they are commonly used when an author wants a subject matter expert like a doctor, attorney, consultant, or other professional person to double-check the information contained in the book. Sometimes beta readers are there to give a bit of general feedback about the book to help the author in the revision process.

One thing to know about beta readers is that they are not professional editors, and you should not use them as a replacement for good editing. Beta readers are just that—readers. While they can and should point out any issues or problems they see with your work, they do not necessarily have the skills or qualifications to tell you how to fix the problems they may encounter with your book. That is where professional editing is invaluable, because a good editor will not only flag what the issues are, but they will also suggest ways you can fix them.

Now that we've covered editing, the next question you may be asking is how do you get your book in print so readers can get their hands on it once all of this is done. How do formatting, printing, and distribution work? And how can you make sure to get your book out there to the right readers? To tackle this, we will dive into understanding the exciting world of book publishing, and I will help you choose your publishing path.

ACCESS THE CODE: EDITING CHEAT SHEET

How do you find the right editor for your book? I made a handy Editing Cheat Sheet to help you navigate this for yourself. To access it in the reader resources section of my website, visit **www.writingcoachla.com/thecode.**

Author Success Story
CHERYL L. WRIGHT

For over two decades, I dreamed of writing a book. After hearing about my life experiences, friends and family would often tell me to write one, and though I tried many times, I never got further than a few pages or short stories. I lacked the direction, strategy, and confidence needed to turn my experiences into something meaningful for others.

That all changed when I joined Ashley's Book Accelerator® program. It seemed like the perfect opportunity to give my dream another shot. But in signing up, I didn't realize how life-changing it would actually be. I learned that the key to success was having a structured plan, something I had always been missing. Ashley's TAP Method immensely simplified the process and gave me the tools I needed to finally organize my ideas into a coherent strategy.

I spent the first part of the program solely on planning and refining the vision for my book, and once the planning phase was complete, writing became so much easier. I was able to write the entire book in just ten weeks, something I never thought possible. After years of struggling to figure out what to write and how to do it, completing it felt like a monumental achievement, and I now have a book I am incredibly proud of.

This has been a life-changing accomplishment for me, as I am now using my book as a launchpad for my career as an author, speaker, and empowerment coach. My mission is to help as many people as I can break free from toxic relationships, rebuild their confidence, and reclaim their self-worth. I'm deeply committed to making a difference in the lives of others, and I know this book is the first step in empowering as many people as possible to reclaim their lives and embrace their true worth.

If you're ready to turn your own story into a powerful book, I highly recommend Ashley's Book Accelerator® and Brands Through Books programs—they have truly made all the difference in bringing my vision to life.

—CHERYL L. WRIGHT, bestselling author
of *Swimming with Alligators*

CHAPTER THIRTEEN

CHOOSING YOUR PUBLISHING PATH

T HE PUBLISHING INDUSTRY has undergone quite a transformation since Gutenberg's printing press of 1440. Today, there are more ways than ever to be published. This is good news for the first-time author who is wondering if they will ever have a shot at seeing their book in print. The answer, of course, is a resounding yes! Anyone can see their book in print today thanks to print-on-demand services like those offered by Amazon, IngramSpark, and others. But seeing your book in print should not be the end goal here. The most exciting aspect of book publishing for the first-time author is getting the book out there to thousands of readers. And to do that successfully, it's important to decide on a publishing path.

You must have a clear publishing path to reach your readers. This is where so many aspiring authors get overwhelmed and quit. They think that because there are a million and one different options for publishing, they won't know which avenue to go with and get frustrated and quit. Don't quit when you are about to reach the top! The good news is when you really break down the publishing industry, it is far less complicated than you might think.

Regardless of what a Google search turns up, the truth is there are only three paths to publishing: self-publishing (including assisted self-publishing, or what we do for authors in Bestseller Legacy, which is what I call full-service self-publishing), hybrid or partner publishing, and traditional publishing. To put it simply, either you are your own publisher and you self-publish, you and a publisher partner split your responsibilities (hybrid publishing), or you let the publisher do mostly everything (traditional publishing). Unfortunately, these days, traditional publishing is starting to look more and more like self-publishing since the author is expected to do more and take on greater responsibilities for their book, especially where marketing is concerned. And self-publishing is beginning to look more and more like traditional publishing, as publishers both large and small sell self-publishing style services to new authors, sometimes as vanity presses. But here's what to know: if you have a publisher on your side (i.e., an outside entity with legitimate staff and support), then you are either in hybrid or traditional publishing. If you don't, you're self-publishing, meaning you are the publisher.

PREDATORY PUBLISHING: A WORD OF CAUTION

When opting to work with a publisher, do your research. Many publishing services out there today are creating a blend of traditional publishing and self-publishing by offering self-publishing services that the author must purchase under the guise of being published under a big-name imprint or publishing house. Whenever fees are being paid to a publisher, you must look at the fine print, especially when those fees are for things like editing, book design, or marketing and launch services and you are contracting with the publisher to print your books under the publisher's imprint. This may be vanity publishing, especially if said publisher is taking a fee *and* retaining rights and royalties. I'm a firm believer that if you are paying a publisher for services, *you* should retain all rights and royalties, because this constitutes self-publishing. In other words, I don't believe it's right for an author to pay a publisher to own their work. In fact, it should be the other way around. If a publisher is retaining rights and royalties, they should be paying you!

Unfortunately, there are far too many self-publishing services out there disguising themselves as publishers and taking advantage of uninformed authors who think that it's normal for a publisher to take your money *and* your rights and royalties. The truth is this constitutes predatory publishing, and you need to be careful. I don't care how fancy the publisher looks or what kind of sweet deal they offer you, please read the fine print and have a literary attorney look anything over before you sign with said publisher. A good attorney will tell you if the deal is in your best interest or not.

CHOOSE YOUR PUBLISHING PATH

Now that we've broken down the world of publishing into three simple paths, the next thing to know here is that you can decide how you want to be published. Yes, it really is in your hands. Most people at this phase of the process mistakenly believe that they don't have a choice or that the choice has been taken from them, but it really is all up to you. Don't let anyone tell you that you are limited as to how you can publish your book. The right publisher is probably out there for you, you just have to find them. Equally, don't let anyone dismiss self-publishing either. Just because you had a friend who self-published and it didn't work out for her doesn't mean it won't work out for you. Your friend likely never read this book and understood these secrets, which is why she's probably still bemoaning the process today. But her result doesn't have to be yours.

When you understand that how you publish your book really is your choice, you can start to do things better. Remember, you have to decide and take action, otherwise nothing ever happens! The good news is there is a really easy way to figure out which publishing path is right for you by answering two questions:

1. How fast do you want to publish?
2. How much control and responsibility do you want to have over the book when you publish?

Let's dive into answering each one.

QUESTION 1: HOW FAST DO YOU WANT TO PUBLISH?

When you think about how fast you want to get your book out there to readers, you are figuring out something called your speed to market, meaning how quickly your book can get to your customers (your ideal readers). In the world of traditional book publishing, the process of getting a book to market can often take years. At the time of writing, for example, I'm witnessing authors not getting their books to market in traditional publishing for upwards eighteen to twenty-four months from the time they sign their contract to their print release. I've heard from some of my sources that books can take as long as thirty-six months or more to publish. That's two to three years for some publishers to release the book *after* you have your contract! When you factor in the time it takes to get an agent, pitch a publisher, and negotiate the contract, you may be looking at anywhere from three to five years.

Can it happen faster and do publishers sometimes push books out quicker than that? Of course. But it's typical for publishers to move more slowly with a first-time author, since first-time authors tend to be higher risk for the publisher. The publisher won't necessarily be willing to expend the resources to get a book to market quickly if the author is deemed to be a riskier investment. They'll want to make sure they get all their ducks in a row, and that can take a heck of a long time! For this reason alone, many aspiring nonfiction authors simply don't want to wait for a traditional publishing deal. Fair enough! You have a book to leverage after all. If you are a fiction writer, however, and traditional publishing has been a dream for a while, then you may not mind waiting and going this route.

In hybrid or partner publishing, the time it takes to get a book to market shrinks dramatically to nine to twelve months from the time of contract. In my experience, hybrid publishers move much faster because they are usually smaller and have more nimble teams and processes. This means your book can get out there faster! The trade-off here is the publisher might not have the level of prestige that many traditional publishers have, and your readers might not have heard of them. If that bothers you, consider the fact that a layperson won't care who your publisher is and likely won't even bother to look. Most readers don't do so unless they are in the book business. You'll have to weigh the pros and cons of trading in a bit of prestige for a faster route to market and the chance to get your book published in a fraction of the time a traditional publisher would take. For this reason, hybrid publishers are the perfect compromise for many aspiring authors.

Now let's look at self-publishing. If you are self-publishing your book, then you can do the entire process, and if you know what you are doing, you can get your book out in a few months. The challenge is that most first-time authors have no idea what they are doing when it comes to self-publishing, which is why you hear so many self-publishing horror stories of books taking forever to get done and ultimately selling very few copies. This is why I created our full-service self-publishing program called Bestseller Legacy, to take the entire task of self-publishing off the shoulders of first-time authors. In our Bestseller Legacy self-publishing program, we do everything for you from start to finish and take care of the editing, book design, typesetting, e-book conversion, and printing and even run the marketing and book launch for you. The wonderful thing is we're able to do almost everything other publishers can do and even some things they can't or won't do, such as creating quality audiobooks and really cool marketing campaigns many traditional publishers would be envious of. On top of that, we're able to get most books out for our authors in about six months, which is half the time hybrids take and about a tenth of the time traditional publishers take.

One of the common questions we get asked is "I get you can do it fast, but what about the quality?" Thankfully, due to print-on-demand methods today and the talent of our team of professional editors and book designers who have decades of experience working in publishing, we are able to create results that are on par or better than what other publishers, both traditional and hybrid, can produce. When an author works with us in Bestseller Legacy, for example, they get bespoke publishing services that rival other top-tier publishers, and the results speak for themselves. Our books never look self-published or low quality, and in fact, they have fooled many people who didn't believe our authors were self-published. This makes full-service self-publishing options like ours a very attractive road for first-time authors because it removes all guesswork from the equation, ensures a high-quality end product, and allows the author to retain all rights and royalties while getting their book to readers in a few months. Pretty amazing, isn't it?

Speed to market is one of the most important decisions a first-time author can make. How fast your book can get out there determines things like how fast you can start profiting and leveraging the book into income-producing channels. The longer the process takes, the more time elapses before you can do this, which means you have to either be very patient or have other ways of growing and marketing your business, attracting new clients, or creating new income opportunities while you wait. Remember, money always replenishes, but time never does, which is why I would opt for the fastest speed to market. It's also why I opted to publish this very book you are reading now through our Bestseller Legacy program.

QUESTION 2: HOW MUCH CONTROL AND RESPONSIBILITY DO YOU WANT TO HAVE OVER THE BOOK WHEN YOU PUBLISH?

Let's talk about the second question you need to answer to decide your publishing path: control and responsibility. Are you a control freak? Do you like to know what is happening every second that your manuscript is being made into a book and micromanage the process? I once knew an author like this. She couldn't let go of the book and trust the production process. She rejected every single cover and ended up designing the whole thing herself in Canva. She tried to micromanage every single detail of the book launch, and as a result, her book fell flat because she didn't listen to the team of professionals she'd hired on things like the cover design, the marketing, or the launch strategy. As a result, the book had very limited success. Sometimes being a control freak doesn't get you the best result. In fact, I would argue that in the world of books, unless you want to self-publish and do everything yourself (meaning, have no expert outside help), then you really should be prepared to collaborate and relinquish some degree of control. For all my control freaks out there, pay attention here. If you feel you need to control the whole process and micromanage everything, you could be compromising your book's quality and its potential to do well when it launches.

If you are someone who wants to retain control but is open to expert input and consultation, then go with self-publishing and hire experts to help you. You may find that you still need to give up some control, but it will be very different than traditional or hybrid publishing where you give up most control and have very little say in what happens with your book. In hybrid publishing, you have a bit more control since you are partnering with your publisher, but in most cases, the publisher still owns the publishing rights to your book and can make big decisions like what the cover should look like, how to price and distribute the book, and even how to market it. That said, you have a lot more control than you do with a traditional publisher, who will virtually control the entire process from start to finish. This is especially true for first-time authors who don't have a track record and no publishing success to point to.

To sum it up, self-publishing is great if you want more control over your project, whereas hybrid and traditional publishing give you far less control because the publisher will mostly be calling the shots and dictate what needs to happen. Remember, when you work with a publisher, you also have a legally binding contract you must adhere to. There may be certain things in the contract you can have input on, but usually, the final say is the publisher's.

Once you answer these two questions for yourself, you'll be able to decide the right publishing path for you. Getting to the next step will require going back to the TAP Method and the foundation you built from day one.

ACCESS THE CODE: YOUR PUBLISHING PATH

For additional help deciding your path, you can access my Publishing Pathways Cheat Sheet in the reader resources section of my website by visiting **www.writingcoachla.com/thecode**.

REBECCA BARKHOUSE

After finding Ashley through Facebook and discussing her Book Accelerator® program, I knew it was exactly what I needed to write the book I had always envisioned but never knew how to accomplish. I went from idea to finished first draft in 90 days! And the TAP Method was the key to my success. By learning that creativity can be measured in bite-size goals, it made writing the draft more possible than it had ever been.

I have a busy life and a short attention span, so the fact that the TAP Method kept the goals short, measurable, and easy to reach was perfect. I truly enjoyed writing my book because it gave me feelings of accomplishment at multiple stretches throughout the process. This kept me encouraged to continue to the end. It's like the TAP Method is a bucket that your creativity just pours into!

The guidance and coaching I received while writing the first draft continued on into my Bestseller Legacy publishing program as well. Every editor and project manager I worked with was so helpful. I always felt comfortable asking questions and knew I was getting honest feedback and insight from some of the best industry experts. I am beyond thrilled with how my published book turned out. It amazes me that I wrote a draft in 90 days and published 6 months later, becoming a bestseller in multiple Amazon categories. It would never have happened without Ashley's two programs and the teams behind them!

It is an overwhelming experience to officially be a bestselling author, but in the very best of ways. When it came time to market and promote my book, my project manager came to my rescue, guiding me along again and encouraging me to just go for it.

Once I started posting about my book, the response and support I received were incredible! I will be using my book to arrange speaking engagements about my work and teachings, as well using it to build the foundation of my new coaching courses. Writing and publishing a book is already proving to be the successful building block I always knew it would be.

—Rebecca Barkhouse, Class 1 flight instructor and bestselling author of *Unlocking Exceptional You*

CHAPTER FOURTEEN

Becoming a Bestselling Author

Do you know the number one reason why most people don't become bestselling authors? It's because they don't think they can do it. Most people are intimidated by the term *bestseller*, and they count themselves out of the opportunity before they even get started. I've made it my mission to understand the art of becoming a bestselling author so I can achieve it for myself and help my author students do the same. There is a lot that goes into it depending on the type of bestseller you want, be it a bestseller on Amazon or in *Publishers Weekly*, Barnes & Noble, *USA Today*, or *The New York Times*. They are all very different, and you need to do different things in order to reach those bestseller lists. The number one thing you need to get started is a strategy.

To become a bestselling author, you need to utilize a foundational strategy like the TAP Method. This is crucial because everything that was important in planning and writing the book becomes even more important when you begin marketing and selling the book. That's why if you do not have a good strategy like the TAP Method when you write the book, you won't have a good basis to think about properly marketing and selling it later. Your strategy is so important because it answers three core questions:

1. Who is the book for?
2. What is the book about?
3. Why does the book matter?

If you cannot answer these questions before you start writing, you will have a very difficult time trying to answer them later on when it's time to market. Answer them up front, then clarify those answers and sharpen them as you go along. By the time you are ready to launch the book and run a bestseller campaign, you will know exactly who you are talking to (target audience and your ideal reader), what message you're sharing with your audience (value proposition or what's in it for them), and the number one reason why they must read your book (the call to action).

The challenge is that most people only think about selling and marketing the book *after* it is already published and it's time to launch it—but by then, it's too late! I encourage you to think well in advance about what your bestseller campaign is going to look like from the beginning of the writing process by having a foundational writing strategy like the TAP Method to help you answer the who, what, and why questions of your book.

When you do this, you can return to the core tenants of the TAP Method. Who are you writing for? What is the book about? Why does it matter? These are the questions you absolutely need to answer clearly well before it's time to get the book to market. This is why the strategy you use when prewriting is the most important factor for your entire journey, because it sets you up to market and sell the book successfully later on.

As you can see, when it comes to writing, publishing, and becoming a bestselling author, the process builds on itself and comes full circle. That's why I encourage you to start off your journey on the right foot and begin with a proper foundation and writing strategy like the TAP Method from day one. When you do, you'll be able to move seamlessly from step one of idea and impulse, the very beginning stage of the book writing and publishing process, all the way to step seven of becoming a bestselling author. The exciting thing to remember is that as soon as you get past step three and finish your first draft, the pearly gates open for you and everything beyond this step becomes possible! Revision, editing, and publishing all become so much easier once the first draft is done and you can actually take a step back and see the book you have written. It's my goal that every aspiring author gets to this critical step and then moves seamlessly to publishing and beyond.

Remember, the first draft is in many ways the most important aspect of the process because with just an idea and no finished draft, you can't do anything else. No editors will work with you, no publishers will care, and no readers will be interested in your unwritten book. You actually have to write the book to get to the next step, which is why step three of writing the first draft is so critical. Make it your sole mission to get there! If you do nothing else, write that first draft! Even if you don't like it, even if you think it's terrible, it doesn't matter. We are our own worst critics, and I promise it's rarely as bad as you might think. Remember, it's called a rough draft for a reason, and once you have it down on paper, you can always make it better. There are many people out there, including me and my team, who can help you polish it, make it wonderful, and get it to market after it's written. But you need to take the first step.

It's so easy *not* to do this, I know. Maybe that's why you're here, reading this book, because you know you need help getting to that next step of your authorship journey. No matter how gifted you are as a writer, no matter how much you know, and no matter how amazing your stories, your expertise, or your message is, none of it matters if you cannot get your book written and out into the world! Step one is to decide to do this, and really do it—to cut yourself off from all other possibilities. Once you do, you must decide if you want to take what we call the ordinary journey or if you want to move at the speed of success with the Book Accelerator® journey.

THE ORDINARY JOURNEY VERSUS THE BOOK ACCELERATOR® JOURNEY

The ordinary journey is when you try to walk this path by yourself. The result looks like this:

THE ORDINARY JOURNEY (WITHOUT STRATEGY AND SUPPORT)

Many people start out with the intention of walking this path alone. Very few, a tiny percentage, actually get to the bestseller, and as you can see in the ordinary journey, many people drop off at each step along the way. Why is that? Typically, they do not have support or someone to help them navigate the various pitfalls at each step. Unless you have walked this path already, it's very difficult to navigate it alone, without a guide. In my own authorship journey, I continuously seek out the help of experts, mentors, and coaches. I know what it's like to try do it alone, and the result was the epic failure of my first book that I shared with you earlier, which took me three years to write and eventually ended up rejected and in my shredder. Had I invested in some help at the start of that process, I know I would not have struggled so much and failed so miserably.

After that experience, I learned my lesson and began seeking out help whenever I could. The first coach I had changed the game and opened my eyes to what was possible for me. She worked with me every single week to help me reach my goals and make the progress I desired. I realized after my next book was finished so much faster and after getting advice and guidance from my coach and other successful writers that you cannot do this journey alone. At that moment, I decided I'd rather go further with someone helping me than travel alone and struggle along the path. Even now as I write this, I am still utilizing the help of experts, mentors, and other authors who have succeeded in ways I still have not. I enjoy the process of learning from them and being coached so I can grow and accomplish even greater feats in both my authorship and my life. That journey will never stop for me, and I invite you to think about your own authorship journey in the same way.

Doing anything well in life requires you to surround yourself with the right people. People who have already succeeded in what you are trying to do. People who have the same ambitions and who you can learn from. This is why I created Book Accelerator®, my 90-day book writing program, because I know that writing in a community with others who aspire as you do and who have great ambitions and big dreams is so much more productive and uplifting than doing this in isolation.

In Book Accelerator®, we guide our author students through the entire process from idea to finished first-draft manuscript. From here, most of our authors return and work with us so we can guide them all the way to publishing and bestselling. It is always a real honor and a gift for us to work with an author to get from idea to bestseller because we get to support them through the entire process from start to finish and then watch as they go on to have amazing careers as authors, speakers, podcasters, influencers, business owners, coaches, consultants, and more. As a result, a much larger percentage of our authors reach their goals when they go through our programs, because we can guide them along the path and help them navigate the crucial challenges that would otherwise stop them. This is why the Book Accelerator® journey looks very different from the ordinary journey, with more authors reaching steps six and seven and doing so happily, quickly, and easily. For us, the fun of the Book Accelerator® journey is knowing that a very high percentage (nearly 100 percent) of authors who enter our program and follow the TAP Method will go on to have amazing careers.

THE BOOK ACCELERATOR JOURNEY (WITH THE RIGHT STRATEGY AND SUPPORT)

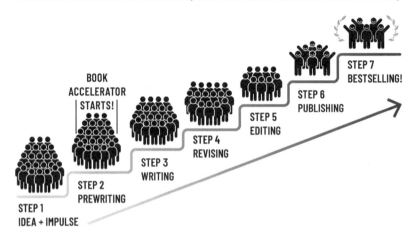

Perhaps you are ready to embark on the journey toward authorship for yourself. If so, you will want to consider getting support with a book writing and publishing program like Book Accelerator®. We are not the only option on the market, but because of our results, track record, world-class team, and proprietary teachings like the TAP Method, I can confidently say our program is recognized as a leader in the book industry and one you should absolutely consider. What I've found is that those who complete Book Accelerator® don't just have immediate success but have a long-lasting legacy as well, meaning what they learn inside our program sticks with them. That's why so many of our authors go on to write and publish multiple books utilizing the TAP Method and everything they have learned.

When you master the TAP Method and have a program like Book Accelerator® to support your writing and publishing goals, the big picture looks something like this:

The exciting thing is you can repeat the process and keep walking the path to publishing once you've done it successfully for the first time, as many of our authors do.

THE BIG PICTURE

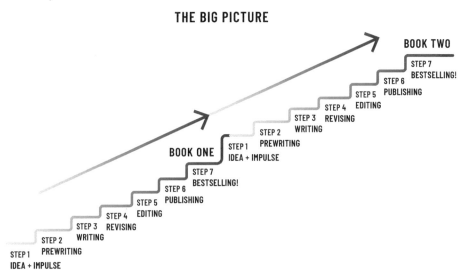

We've now covered the seven steps to writing and publishing a bestselling book, but what if I told you there is a secret final step we haven't talked about yet? The secret step is all about not only becoming a bestseller but profiting from your book too. As I mentioned earlier, when you understand the entire TAP Method and you utilize it to write your book, you are set up to market and sell it. You are also setting yourself up to earn a substantial profit from your book in more ways than you can imagine. In the next chapter, I will show you how.

ACCESS THE CODE: BECOME A BESTSELLER

Want more insight into what it takes to become a bestseller? I created a Bestseller FAQs PDF guide to help you. To access it in the reader resources section of my website, visit
www.writingcoachla.com/thecode.

LOUISE DAVIS

My goal has always been to become a full-time published fiction author. With Ashley's TAP Method, I was able to write the first draft of my first novel in just eighteen days. Then, thanks to her Publishing Master program, I secured a publishing contract with a traditional publisher. I used Ashley's TAP Method again to write my second novel, which my publisher also offered a contract for, and it was published the next year. The full-time author dream is rapidly becoming a reality!

Joining a community and network of authors that I met through social media after publishing my first novel has been a huge blessing in my life. We uplift one another and provide beta reading and feedback that is so helpful. It is a community I never could have joined or confidently contributed to without finding the success of publishing first. I have had the opportunity to be interviewed on podcasts, was asked to be a panelist at a live author event, and had the pleasure of speaking at an elementary school and a high school about my author journey.

My debut novel hit #1 in two different Amazon new release categories and #1 in Amazon's teen and young adult clean and wholesome romance category—an extremely competitive one! I had launch parties for both novels where I read their prologues and signed books. It was such a surreal and incredible experience to do these things that "real" authors get to do. Thanks to Ashley, I'm becoming one of those people I used to look up to, and I can hardly believe it!

—LOUISE DAVIS, bestselling author
of *Haunted by You* and *My Haunted Vow*

NOAH KITTY

After retiring from thirty years as a pulpit rabbi, I wanted to spend what time I had left with the most focus and intentionality I could muster. I just needed to decide what I wanted my life to be, then figure out how to make it happen.

I floundered for several years until I came across Ashley Mansour, who had developed a brilliantly effective way for people who had something to say to finally get their words on paper, then get that paper published. She called it the TAP Method, and when I joined her Book Accelerator® program to learn it, my eyes were finally opened to my own cause and intentions.

If you commit to fully trusting Ashley and her process, the TAP Method really works. I wrote my book from start to finish in just seven weeks. By that point, I was all-in on Ashley and her team, so I committed to publishing my book by joining Brands Through Books. I was confident her team would help me achieve what I knew I couldn't do on my own, and that confidence paid off.

Now that I'm a published author with an empowering message to share, I am scheduling local speaking gigs and creating outlets like a website and videos to help promote my message, which is to understand that just because antisemitism exists doesn't mean you have to feel bad or sad because a total stranger wants you to. I am so eager to continue sharing this message with the world, and now I have the platform I need to do so.

I believe most people have a story to tell that could help others with their struggles, teach a profitable skill, or provide delightful entertainment to lift hearts and spirits. Ashley Mansour, her programs, and her team, are an excellent platform for helping people to realize just how true that is.

—NOAH KITTY, bestselling author of *Thank You, Antisemites*

BECOME A MASTER OF MONEY

CHAPTER FIFTEEN

The 7th Secret

Become a Master of Money

Looking back at my childhood, I can see I was a budding entrepreneur from a very early age. Growing up, I would frequently
come up with business ideas. I had a $1 car wash business, a $1
babysitting business, and even a $1 potions business (don't ask). My best
customers, though, came when I learned to raise my prices. Babysitting
eventually went from $5 an hour to $10, then $20 or more per hour as
I got older and became known in the neighborhood as the responsible
babysitter families could trust. Making $20 per hour back then was a lot
of money to me. With $20 in my pocket, it felt like I could conquer the
world! Really, it meant I could go to the movies or get a burger and milk-
shake with my friends. What felt exciting to me was that I didn't have to
ask anyone for money to do the things I wanted to do, and if my friends
didn't have money, I could pay their way. I thought that was pretty cool.
The value of having money for me was the independence and autonomy
it gave me. This was an important gift and step in my journey to becoming an entrepreneur because what I realized was that with money, I had
more freedom to do the things I wanted to do in life and the ability to
help others along the way.

When I started my own coaching business, I began to see the same
thing play out. At first, I wasn't making much of a profit, but after I raised
my prices and began to attract the students I most wanted to work with,
the $20 in my pocket grew to $20,000, then $40,000 per month, and now

to much more. This revenue we generate in the business allows me to support my team and help them grow, support my family, have the freedom and independence to do what I want when I want, and create the impact I desire in the world by helping others. With profit in your pocket, you can do the same and not only improve your life for yourself and your loved ones but also have the amazing experiences you want in life while helping others along the way.

Unfortunately, while many aspiring authors have the desire for freedom and independence and would love to help others, not many authors understand how important mastering money is. This is especially true when it comes to making money from books. We are taught that we should starve and suffer for our art and that to be commercially minded is distasteful or unseemly. We (especially females) are often taught not to speak of money at all. But the profitable author is far better offer than the bankrupt one. Why? Because the profitable author can afford to keep writing and doing all the other important things they desire to do in life, including providing for others and continuing to share their message with the world!

Think about it. If you are making money from your books, you will have the time to keep writing them, publishing them, and promoting them. If they are profitable, of course you will write more and more and more. The profitable author can work for herself. She can become her own boss, manage her own time, and create what she wants when she wants. She can be an entrepreneur, sometimes called an authorpreneur. There is no stopping this author because she can make money doing what she loves most in the world while helping others and living a free, independent life along the way. How many people can actually claim that?

To become a profitable author is to give yourself freedom, time, capacity, and space. It is to give yourself the opportunity to command your life and live freely and independently. It also gives you the opportunity to put good back into the world through your books, your courses, your talks and seminars, and everything you create. Who wouldn't desire that?

We talked about how to write the book and what the path toward publishing looks like, but now let's turn our attention to how you become that profitable author once you write it. We must turn our focus toward money so I can show you how your first book can dramatically increase your income and your earning power forever, if you understand the secret of becoming a master of money.

DON'T BELIEVE WHAT THE NAYSAYERS TELL YOU

At some point on this journey, you will hear someone clear their throat and very proudly tell you, "You don't make money from books." When this happens, I want you to pause and gather yourself. Do not take this as truth right away. I want you to think to yourself, *Gee this person must not have made money from their books*, and then get curious. Ask them about their experience with publishing a book, and you will soon discover why they hold this belief. Once you've heard their account, discard it completely. It isn't yours. Just because they failed at becoming profitable doesn't mean you will too. Remember, because you hold this book and the secrets herein, you are in the perfect position to not only write and publish a great bestselling book but to earn handsomely from it too.

The phrase "you don't make money from books" is the number one misconception about books and money. The misconception is perpetuated by those who do not understand book economics. By book economics, I'm talking about how one actually earns an entire living from their books and becomes a profitable author.

BOOK ECONOMICS

The first thing to understand about book economics is that book sales don't make you rich. Yes, I do realize the name of the game is to actually sell books, and yes, this is important. I have sold tens of thousands of books in my career, so I understand. It matters. But I never made significant money from book sales alone. The tired notion of worrying about individual book sales ought to be thrown out the window. It's a distraction, but one that pulls many aspiring authors' focus as they embark on the business side of authorship. Perhaps you don't think you are in business as an author, but the truth is when you become an author, you are absolutely in the book business as well as the knowledge, education, and even entertainment business.

Many new authors focus on individual book sales and the money they can make from simply selling books. They do the math and then worry they will never be able to pay their bills, let alone themselves, with the slim checks they get in the mail. Regardless of whether you publish yourself or have a publisher to help you, you will never get 100 percent of the retail price of the book. You will always have to pay someone their cut for something, whether that's your printer, your publisher, your distributor, or someone else.

But what if I told you the secret to becoming a profitable author is not to worry about individual sales? What If I told you that you are thinking about book economics all wrong and that the secret to becoming a profitable author means changing the way you think about your book forever?

After my first book came out, things were going very well. I was selling a lot of books, and I quickly became a bestselling author in the US and internationally. But after some time, the sales began to slow down, and I wasn't making nearly as much as when I'd started. So I did what I saw other authors doing and attempted to sell more books. I did school visits, book fairs, signings, and any type of book-related event I could find.

One hot summer day, my husband and I loaded up our truck with a bunch of books and supplies and made our way to a local book fair. We set up shop, and as the sun rose in the sky, so did the heat and the pressure to start making sales. At first, things were slow, so I started walking around and talking to readers, and sure enough, they'd come back to the booth and buy a copy of my book. I was excited, but I knew we had to keep selling despite the hundred-degree heat.

Time ticked on, I kept selling books, and soon it became apparent we only had a few minutes left before we'd have to close up shop, pack up, and go home. I pushed hard, selling books as fast as I could, eager to turn a profit at the event. By the time the last book was sold, I was exhausted, sweaty, and drained. I remember checking with my husband and asking him, "How much have we made?"

"About $235."

"What?" I was shocked. "I thought it was more than that."

No sooner did he say that than a young boy approached the tent and bought the last copy of my book to be sold that day for $15.

I was momentarily happy with our grand total of $250. And then I remembered. We had paid $250 for our booth. All we did was break even!

My heart sank. All that work in the heat for nothing! To make matters worse, we hadn't even covered our gas money or made enough to cover paying ourselves something for our time. I felt defeated and totally beaten down. It was one of the most humbling moments of my life.

Sadly, my story isn't unique. This is the experience of many first-time and even seasoned authors who are taught an insufficient model of making money from their books. But there is a far better way to have a career as an author, to make money, to profit, and to become a master of money.

MY $5,000 EPIPHANY

Before I share with you the key moment that changed the way I think about monetizing books forever, I'd like to ask you one thing: do you still believe books don't make money? If so, I challenge you to do a little self-inventory. Where did that belief come from? Why do you believe what you do? Did someone pass it on to you? Is it yours through an experience like mine at the book fair? Whatever the reason, it's good to see it, know it, and then understand this one thing: you can choose to form a new belief.

My new belief formed through an experience that taught me the secret that becoming a successful and profitable author does not come from only selling books and relying on royalties. One warm spring afternoon, I spent a few hours updating my LinkedIn profile and added my bestselling book to my profile. I decided to message some contacts and make a few new connections. A few days later, I received a message from a new connection. In the message was an invitation to work as a consultant on a project. At first, I was a little confused. Nothing quite made sense because they were offering me two weeks of work for $5,000! I had never been offered money like that before, and it couldn't have been a better time, as bills were coming due and I needed to generate income fast. This one amazing moment sparked something in me.

After I met with the company, signed the contract, and began working for them, I began to realize how important this moment was. When the $5,000 payment landed in my bank account, I knew my life had changed forever. Later, I decided to ask the person I was working for why he'd hired me in the first place in hopes of repeating the experience.

"Oh," he said thoughtfully. "We found your book, read it, and really liked it, and we knew we wanted to hire you right away."

My book had made this big company want to hire me because they'd read my words and loved my message! It felt amazing and so gratifying to know my work had landed me this opportunity to make $5,000 in a couple of weeks. And, because I was consulting, there were no royalties, no publisher, and no agent to take a cut. On top of that, I had no fixed/hard costs. I simply gave my creative input, my time, and my expertise to this company in exchange for money. And this wasn't a one-off deal; opportunities like this started coming in all the time—from writers willing to pay me to help them with their projects, companies asking for my expertise, consulting gigs, and businesses wanting to partner with me to create content for them. Before I knew it, I was being paid handsomely for my expertise and my knowledge. It felt like the world had opened up and I was once again that kid with $20 in my pocket, ready to take on the world!

This whole new world of possibility helped me learn a very important lesson. I now know this is the most important principle you can ever learn about making money from books. This is the secret, one I want you to internalize now and forever: making money from books happens when you stop focusing on selling your book and start focusing on *leveraging* your book instead.

ACCESS THE CODE: MONEY MASTERY

Want to master money quickly? I created a Money Mastery Worksheet to help you get started. To access it in the reader resources section of my website, visit ***www.writingcoachla.com/thecode****.*

Author Success Story
HEATHER BROWNE

Ashley has shown me that writing a book can open so many doors and lead to so many incredible experiences, all because you decide to say "yes" to sharing your message and seeing that goal through.

So much has happened for me since publishing my book about transforming relationships! I've been approached to speak at events and to write as an expert for a youth website, and I've made three different television appearances as well as been a guest on over fifty podcasts to speak about the importance of compassionate communication.

I have also been able to increase my service rate for my business by 20 percent because of my new notoriety. And I now have international clients reaching out to work with me, all ready to sign up and pay in full! People who would never have known about me are now asking to work together. All of this has happened because of people reading and growing from my book.

But most importantly, writing and publishing my book has opened the door of my heart. I am so pleased to have given myself a voice, to have empowered myself to share, and to have forged unbelievably beautiful connections with followers who have deepened my call and passion for helping this world learn how to care, connect, and begin by speaking with the heart.

—Dr. Heather Browne, PsyD, LMFT, psychotherapist, TEDx speaker, and bestselling author of *Speaking with the Heart*

GAYE KICK

Ashley's Book Accelerator® and Bestseller Legacy programs really can work for anyone and any type of book! I wanted to write a memoir for years but just couldn't figure out how to put all my ideas together into a cohesive book. The Book Accelerator® program helped me resolve that in a fraction of the time it was taking to achieve on my own.

The publishing journey with Ashley's team was a wonderful one, and my memoir turned out so beautifully. Not to mention, it became a bestseller! My book has enabled me to engage with blogs and appear as a guest on shows and at book events to talk about my life and share the lessons found in my book.

I've had several renowned bloggers, interviewers, and podcast hosts feature my book and story on their websites and shows, which has increased the reach and readership of not just my book but my blog. I was even invited to my local author expo event for a book signing, which was an incredible experience.

My book is now available on Amazon and the Target and Walmart websites and is even available in the biography section of my local Barnes & Noble, as well as in my local library. There is nothing quite like seeing your published book sitting on bookstore and library shelves. None of this would have happened without the help of Ashley and her team.

—GAYE KICK, bestselling author of *Releasing Religion: A Minister's Wife Goes Rogue*

CHAPTER SIXTEEN

The PAE System and the Power of Leverage

I MAGINE FOR a moment that each and every copy of your book that is bought, sold, and read is like an expert sales and marketing professional making their rounds in the world, impacting people one by one and convincing them to purchase your programs, products, or services. The best part is that you pay this sales and marketing professional no salary. They never need training to do their job well. They act and sound like you and uphold all your values. And they always, without question, deliver your message powerfully and professionally. That is the powerful leverage a great book can have in the world. When I say you need to leverage your book, what I mean is you need to leverage the authority, credibility, and clout it brings you to create valuable and lucrative opportunities. I mean letting your book do the heavy lifting for you to attract these opportunities. If you understand the power of leverage, your book can be the single best sales and marketing tool for you, your brand, your business, and your income you will ever have.

You may be thinking, *But I don't have a business!* Remember, if you have a book and you are an author, you have a business. The business of authorship and the business of books is one I recommend you embrace regardless of your genre. As an author, you will have a brand, you will earn income and opportunities from said brand, and you will be expected to participate in the marketing and sales side of your author-ship business. With that said, it's important to embrace this new way of thinking if you haven't yet and celebrate the fact that your books can increase your earning potential many times over.

MORE THAN A BUSINESS CARD

One thing I often hear people say is, "Having a book is the best business card." But a book is so much more than a business card that winds up in the trash. Books take up space in our homes, on our shelves, tables, and nightstands. We take them with us when we travel, when we go to sleep at night, when we are knee-deep in a new project. Books become part of our daily lives; business cards become part of our daily garbage.

Books, as you have seen, can also be very lucrative. That's why I encourage you not to think of your book as just a business card! Through the principles I'm about to teach you, you will learn that a book is actu-ally a debit card to someone else's bank account! And guess what? The account is bottomless. You can keep returning to the ATM over and over again, extracting as much money as you like. Next up, I will show you how this works and the system that's helped me create multiple seven fig-ures of revenue on the backs of my books and helped my author students routinely generate five, six, and seven figures of income from theirs. You can do this too. I'm excited for you to learn how because I know it will change the game for you forever.

THE PAE SYSTEM

If you use the TAP Method to write, you must use the PAE System to profit. What does PAE stand for? It stands for the three things that you must do in order to leverage your book and get *paid* as an author. Remember, TAP to write, PAE to profit and get paid. These three elements of the PAE System create significant leverage and help you command all sorts of exciting new income and revenue opportunities from your book. They help you establish profitable channels from your book so you can maximize your earning power and avoid unprofitable activities like my break-even booth at the book fair.

PAE stands for *positioning, assets,* and *engine.* Let's break the system down step by step so you can apply this to your book too and start earning what you deserve. And do you want to know something powerful and exciting? You can use the PAE System to monetize your book *before* you've even finished writing it. Yes, it's true, and my authors do this every single day! Allow me to show you how this works.

THE PAE SYSTEM: POSITIONING

What is positioning? To put it simply, it's the way you position yourself and your book in the market. Let's take my $5,000 contract, for example. When I put my bestselling book on LinkedIn, I was positioning myself, even though I didn't know it at the time. I thought I was merely updating my social media account. Positioning can take a variety of forms: what you write on your posts and other people's posts; the photos and videos you share; your profiles, channels, accounts, and the content you produce across the internet; your personal branding; and yes, even the way you show up as an author in the world. All of that is part of your positioning as an author. For many, good positioning means being seen as an expert authority, someone who is professional, intelligent, and accomplished. Of course, a book (especially a bestseller) helps tremendously with this. So does the way you present yourself as an author and the way your book is written and published. For others, good positioning might mean being seen as relatable, funny, or controversial. Can you see why it's so critical to have a book that positions you, your brand, and your business in the right way?

To better understand your own market positioning right now, ask yourself a few key questions:

1. Is my positioning right now optimized to maximize my income potential? (i.e., Could I earn more if my positioning were more authoritative, credible, or trustworthy?)
2. Would I want to hire myself for my expertise or skills after looking at my positioning?
3. What does my positioning say about me, my brand, and my book(s)?
4. What will my target audience need to see in my brand positioning to value me and my work at a premium?
5. What am I well-positioned to help others with and what problems does my positioning suggest I can solve for people as an expert?

If you don't like the answers to these questions, don't worry. You can change your positioning. You can even improve it! In fact, you should improve and optimize it over time. To optimize your positioning, there are a few factors you must consider.

- Professionalism: Your level of perceived professionalism in the market.
- Expertise: Your perceived skill or knowledge in a particular field.
- Profile: How you describe and represent who you are and what you do to your target audience.
- Bio and Background: The brief account of your life and expertise, constructed to maximize your value and highlight your achievements.
- Search Engine Results: What content about you appears online when your name is entered in a search engine and how easy you are to locate online.

- Internet Presence: How and where your content, accolades, information, and achievements appear online and how they are presented.
- Personal Brand: The conscious and deliberate presentation of you and your work to influence public perception and position you as an expert authority in your area.

Positioning starts with your book and the way you approach the content. If you follow the secrets I've taught you in this book, you will be well-positioned and already on the path to creating a bestseller. Having this important accolade will help you stand out in what is a crowded marketplace and appeal to your ideal reader's desire to read a great book written by a great author.

To become a bestselling author, you may need to hire someone who knows about bestseller book marketing to help you with your book launch marketing campaign. I do not recommend trying to figure this out yourself, especially with your first book. Instead, get help from trusted experts who can guide you. For example, you can get help with becoming a bestselling author in our full-service Bestseller Legacy publishing program, where we can help you hit bestseller status on Amazon, Barnes & Noble, *USA Today*, and other lists as well. For more information on this, you can visit our website and even download our free guide to becoming a bestselling author from our reader resources page. Visit *www.writingcoachla.com/thecode* to get free access to this and all the other awesome resources offered in this book.

As you begin your positioning campaign, remember that your book is like a piece of real estate. You are very much like a real estate agent who must maximize your property's curb appeal. All areas of the book must be utilized and are important, including the cover, the spine, and the front and back matter. Use these spaces wisely to highlight aspects of your personal brand or business that will appeal to the ideal reader. Consider everything from the cover art to your brand colors and the way the images on the cover look and feel. Hire a good book cover designer and a good interior designer, typesetter, and printer. Make sure your name stands out. Have a clear and compelling book description and author bio. Include your website and any webhooks that are important for you, your career, or your business. Don't shy away from promoting what you do and directing your readers to further resources. It's so important that you utilize each and every element of the book to position yourself properly.

Once you position yourself and the book properly and run your bestseller campaign, take stock of your positioning and answer the questions that were shared earlier in this chapter. Hopefully your answers are far better than the first time around. If not, keep working on your positioning to maximize your income potential and your earning power.

To learn more about positioning and how to position yourself well as an author, download my Author Positioning 101 PDF guide from the reader resources section of my website: *www.writingcoachla.com/thecode*.

THE PAE SYSTEM: ASSETS

Assets are the most exciting part of the PAE System because they are where the value gets created. An asset is a proprietary service, product, or program that makes you money. Assets are so-called because they make you money, and you can always leverage them to earn income or revenue in your business. The great news is once you write your book, there are hundreds of hidden assets waiting for you in the content. Some examples of the most popular assets include:

- Online courses/video courses/self-study courses
- Blueprints/guides/checklists
- Workbooks or companion guides
- Blogs/articles/essays
- Newsletters

- Membership programs
- Coaching programs
- High-ticket programs or services
- Consulting services
- Masterminds and roundtables
- Podcasts
- Keynotes or signature presentations

The list goes on. Many people worry they will have to create all these assets from scratch, but the truth is if you write your book using the TAP Method, you will have a structure and content that can easily be turned into any of these assets. In other words, once you've done the hard work of writing your book once, all you need to do is translate it into another form or medium. For example, once you create the outline, structure, and content of your book with the TAP Method, it's very easy to turn that into a digital course or a signature talk. You can also splice up the content for a paid newsletter or host a high-ticket mastermind or weekly coaching program and use your book as the program curriculum. The possibilities are endless! Think of your book as a bible, codifying everything you know and want to convey to your readers. Once you have it written, you can easily take that content and turn it into any other asset you like!

Why are assets so important? Because you must have something beyond the book to monetize. If you don't, you will be making the key mistake many authors make by believing that because you have a book to sell, you are in the retail business. Remember, as an author, you are not in the retail business; you are in the knowledge and entertainment business! The sooner you understand this, the sooner you will understand that your reader isn't buying from you to simply obtain another physical rectangular object that they can store on a shelf somewhere. Know that your reader is buying from you because of the knowledge, education, and entertainment you provide.

When you understand this key fact, you can start to get serious about providing value for your readers. Ultimately, you want to have positioning and assets so powerful that the reader cannot help but come to you for more than your book. This is the beginning of the PAE System working. But there is more. You need to drive the momentum forward with powerful marketing and promotions. You are mistaken if you think your publisher will continuously drive your book forward and bring you new readers. They will not. In fact, the author is always the sole driving force of the book, even in traditional publishing.

THE PAE SYSTEM: ENGINE

Now that you understand your book is a powerful vehicle that will bring you opportunities to get in front of readers and present them with your many assets, next up, you need something to drive the vehicle forward and help you reach new readers. You must have a marketing engine.

The marketing engine creates momentum and gets your book in front of new readers. You always need your engine to be running. If your engine stops, the vehicle cannot run, your assets do not sell, and you will not make money. If you keep your engine running and take care of it, it will take care of you. When it comes to your book, there are technically two types of engines: your inside engine and your outside engine.

Your inside engine is the marketing and advertising you do inside of the book to promote your assets and send your readers to your offerings, whether free or paid. The engine inside the book can be anything from a sample chapter of your next book at the very end to bonus guides, resources, and worksheets at the back. It can be as simple as listing your website or course information or giving the reader a way to find you on social media. The more commercially minded authors do this very well and also plant hooks inside the material to drive readers toward their assets. For example, in earlier chapters, I mentioned my Book Accelerator® program (paid) as well as reader resources (free) to allow you (my ideal reader) to access more support from me. I mention these because they are core assets of my business. I've shared Book Accelerator® multiple times because I know it is responsible for having the most significant impact for aspiring authors and changes the most lives because of how many authors it has helped. I know two things: 1) the program isn't right for everyone and 2) the right people will know it's the way for them and naturally seek out more information. This is part of my marketing engine, driving readers to visit my website (www.writingcoachla. com/programs) to find out about my programs.

Let me give you another example. The book I am reading right now has three free resources at the back of the book. This is not by accident; it is by design. The engine is driving the book to be read more widely so that it will be taken up by book circles, reading groups, and even schools. The author also has a "hire me to speak" option on his website. Can you see how the inside engine is promoting his speaking? While not every book group will ask him to come and speak, the right people will naturally seek him out to do so. It's a perfect asset and inside engine.

But notice that his inside engine isn't working alone. He also has the outside engine working on his website and social media. In fact, when you go to any of his profiles, you see this author also has snippets of himself speaking professionally to various groups. This is part of his outside engine. The outside engine includes the marketing and advertising activities you do outside the content of the book to make people aware of you, the book, and your other assets.

Perhaps you are like many first-time authors and feel you are not good at marketing. If so, that's okay! The beauty of becoming an author is that you can learn. Marketing yourself and your book is an essential skill to master, and the good news is it's not that complicated once you begin. You can learn this, and once you do, you will be on the leading edge of your industry. Don't be the person who ends up doing nothing at all because they don't know what to do. That's not a solution! Get support. Learn from experts to master marketing and put your best foot forward. You can do this, and it's not as difficult as it might seem. Many of our author students in the Book Accelerator® program start out worried about marketing but quickly find through learning the TAP Method that half the battle is knowing the answers to the top three questions (Who are you writing for? What are you writing about? And why does it matter?) and then sharing those answers repeatedly with others.

So, what does marketing consist of exactly? Well, there are a million ways to market yourself and your book. In the next chapter, we'll cover a few easy ideas that are freely available to you right now.

ACCESS THE CODE: PAE SYSTEM CHEAT SHEET

*If you'd like ideas for powerful positioning, simple, proven assets you can create from your book, and clever marketing, grab my PAE System Cheat Sheet from the reader resources section of my website at **www.writingcoachla.com/thecode**.*

Author Success Story
KEL CAL

I had a vision of writing a book for years before I ever actually wrote it. At the time, I had never really considered working with a writing coach, but a friend of mine spoke so highly of this particular program they were going through called Book Accelerator®. I was intrigued, so I scheduled a call to connect with Ashley Mansour and learn more.

From the very first moment we spoke, I realized she was the support I didn't even know I needed in order to bring my book to life. I signed up for Book Accelerator® immediately after the call and was so excited to begin my writing journey. After that first coaching call, I began to feel the excitement and passion for my purpose and my book amidst the stress, anxiety, and overwhelm I was feeling in every other part of my life. I decided to trust the alignment I felt and commit to the program, and I am so grateful I did, because I completed my manuscript in less than eight weeks!

You hear about writers experiencing writer's block and the writing journey being tedious, frustrating, and even painful at times, but my experience was the exact opposite because I had Ashley's TAP Method framework and support. I loved every second of writing my book because I had the resources and mindset tools to navigate any resistance, which kept me from getting stuck. To this day, people are shocked when I tell them that I wrote my book in eight weeks, but it honestly felt so natural!

I decided to self-publish my book with Ashley's team at Brands Through Books because I wanted their ongoing support and expertise. Could I have published on my own? Of course. But I didn't want to! I had such an amazing experience in Book Accelerator® and wanted to have continuing expertise and guidance so I could devote my energy to my business and other areas of my life rather than learn how to create the wheel from scratch.

My book launched to bestseller status on Amazon, and Ashley's team even set me up to make my book available in local stores where I live in Bali. Seeing my book come to life has been one of the greatest gifts. The internal shifts I experienced on this journey to becoming a bestselling author have impacted every area of my life and have amplified my trust and confidence in myself.

—KEL CAL, empowerment coach, speaker, and bestselling author of *How I Cured My Resting Bitch Face*

CHAPTER SEVENTEEN

Author Marketing 101

W HEN I WROTE my first book, it is fair to say I was no marketer. And yet with a few simple tools and the willingness to share my book writing and publishing journey, I quickly grew an audience of over ten thousand people, landed a book deal, and had my book optioned for film and television. Regardless of whether you consider yourself a marketer, you can do the same, and it doesn't need to be difficult. Let me show you what I mean.

Author marketing starts with understanding that the first goal is to build a readership. That means you have to start sharing your book writing and publishing journey early on. When I did this with my first book, I began posting photos, blog articles, and stories online, sharing what I was working on and giving readers a little taste of my book and my journey as a writer as the manuscript was taking shape. I'll admit that doing this the first few times was nerve-wracking because not only had I never shared much about myself online before, but the book wasn't even finished yet. I was still writing and hoping that this time it would turn out differently than the time before when my manuscript ended up in my shredder.

The good news is I quickly saw my courage pay off, and readers flocked to my Instagram account as I began to open up about who I was writing for, what my book was about, and why I thought it mattered. Soon, I had attracted over ten thousand fans and readers who were excited about my upcoming book.

Some experts in the book industry call this type of promotion guerrilla marketing because it's free, organic, and relatively simple to do.[17] Anyone can become a powerful guerrilla marketer of their own book, just like I did! Doing this successfully requires two things: 1) starting early, ideally when you begin writing, and 2) sharing often, openly, authentically, and with enthusiasm. If you can do these two things, you will find you are able to attract a powerful readership long before your book gets published. This is powerful because with said readership, you can easily calculate how many books you can sell at launch and decide to self-publish or work with a publisher (who will be very glad you chose them to work with because of your large audience).

My own marketing journey led me to have an amazing career as an author and not only allowed me to get published but helped me later on to build a business, since many of my fans and readers eventually became my author students and opted to join my writing programs, like Book Accelerator®. Can you see how important it is to understand your own marketing engine and get it in place from day one of your authorship journey? If you feel nervous to start and are worried about sharing your own book in the early days of writing it, I encourage you to start slowly and build up your courage muscle over time. If you need to, begin by sharing with your friends and family. Then perhaps try posting online in one of the communities or networks you're a part of. After that, experiment with weekly public posts or newsletters and increase the frequency of your posting to your comfort level. You will have to experiment with what works best for you and your target audience. But remember, it's never too early to start your marketing engine and attract future readers to you!

Today, there are a great many free and paid tools at your disposal to help you market and promote your book. It might be overwhelming to think about all the things you should have as a new author, so I want to take the pressure off and share with you the top three online tools you should utilize to begin marketing yourself. Remember, these are a few of the essentials to help you get started quickly and easily.

TOOL NUMBER 1: SOCIAL MEDIA

There are plenty of social media apps, and your ideal reader is very likely on one or more of them and using them daily. Get out there and find them! All social media platforms have ways of grouping audiences. Whether it's hashtags, channels, profiles, groups, or watch parties, it doesn't matter. Your ideal readers are in what I call a cluster of behavior. They are all doing similar, if not the same, things on social media and likely following and interacting with many of the same people or accounts. So go in search of them. Play detective and see what you can find. After you find out where your readers are hanging out and who they are following, you can start creating content to put yourself in front of them. If you're at a loss for how to do this, a simple internet search will turn up tons of free resources to help you figure out where to start. Many of them are located on social media, so you will be actively learning new skills and researching your platform at the same time.

When I did this marketing exercise for my first book, I quickly discovered there were thousands of reading groups and accounts for my target readers. They were known as bibliophiles and bookstagrammers on Instagram. Basically, they were avid readers online who loved books and had turned their Instagram accounts into pretty book devotionals—hence the name bookstagrammers. Once I found them and began engaging with them, thousands of readers flocked to me right away. It was the most magical experience ever because I discovered that the right activities online could make a world of difference to my bottom line. I brought in more readers and then had the opportunity to not only sell them my books but to start leveraging my books into the assets I now have in my business. You can do the same.

TOOL NUMBER 2: A WEBSITE

Let's talk for a moment about your website, or your lack thereof if you don't have one yet. If you don't, that's okay, but this is the time to get one. You can get a website fairly quickly and easily, and you don't need to know how to code or be a web designer to create one. A simple search will turn up tons of free and paid options to get your website up and running quickly.

An author's website is an important tool because you can do a couple of critical things: 1) you can optimize it with useful content and 2) you can use it to attract readers. Optimizing your site isn't difficult. You can simply hire someone to come in and do SEO (search engine optimization) so your site ranks more highly in search engines. If you want to get fancier, you can create content exclusively for this purpose so your site has content that promotes it to the top of various searches that relate to what you do and who you are. For example, if your book is about parenting, then you may have an article about bedtime routines that attracts readers and frequent visitors to your site. This is known as content marketing. It's a way of using internet traffic to pull people to your content (engine) and entice them to make a purchase with you when they buy something (one of your assets). Eventually, you will want to promote your book on your website and have it appear at the very top, with an option for readers to learn more about it, buy it, and get something awesome related to it for free in exchange for their name and email address. When you have this kind of freebie (known as a lead magnet), you're able to build an email list of readers you can communicate with and market your assets to. Remember that when you or your publisher lists your book for sale online and people buy it, you will not be provided any data (like names and email addresses) about those readers. Therefore, you will need to collect your own data and build your own reader email list from your website and other online offerings.

TOOL NUMBER 3: A FUNNEL

Have you ever heard of a marketing funnel? I'm always surprised to learn how many people haven't. A funnel is not a website. It's a specific online sales tool designed to funnel people who land on it into a product or service and convert them into leads or buyers. When you land on someone's funnel, you typically have very few options. You can read the information, sometimes watch a video, and usually click a button that allows you to opt in for whatever the product or freebie is in exchange for your name and email address. A funnel has limited options because it is designed to either get you to click for more or close the page and leave. If you click, it means you are interested and usually on the path to becoming a buyer. A funnel is designed to increase engagement, opt-ins, and purchases. If you have spent any significant time online and clicked on someone's ad, link, or promotion, you have most likely encountered a funnel at some point.

A funnel is also a way of moving a lead or customer through a business's ascension ladder. An ascension ladder is what introduces and brings the customer into the fold of the business through various tiers of free and paid offers. Have you ever gotten a free thing in exchange for your name and email address and then, before you knew it, you were getting out your credit card to buy the $47 thing or the $197 thing? Yep, that is a funnel and a business ascension ladder at work. The good news is they are highly effective and anyone can have a funnel! There are a lot of tools and experts out there who can help you create funnels, and you can find our recommendations in the reader resources section of our website at *www.writingcoachla.com/thecode*.

There are many more things you can consider for your marketing engine, but right now, I encourage you to keep it simple. Get your social media accounts going, get a website and funnel up and running, and then you can start to add to your engine as you move closer to publishing and launching your book into the world. You can do everything from media appearances and podcast interviews to local book signings, events online and offline, traditional PR support, paid promotions and advertising, giveaways and contests, and more. The sky truly is the limit! The important thing is that you keep your marketing engine running and explore new ways to reach new readers. There are many ways to do so and put your marketing engine on autopilot. For example, if you are running ads or doing SEO, much of the time, you won't need to do anything at all to bring people to you. The important thing is to have something in place now that can keep running while you write and publish your book so you can be ready with a waiting readership and audience when your book eventually comes out. Start early, share consistently, and you will continue to attract readers, convert them to your assets, and become the profitable author you desire to be.

CASE STUDY: 5,000 FREE BOOKS, $250,000 IN SALES

I used the PAE System with my first nonfiction book, *The Writer's Success Code*. It was a small book, but it was small for a reason. I wanted people to actually read it cover to cover and put the teachings into practice. For this reason, I also included exercises and a planner they could use to plan out their entire book in seven days using aspects of the TAP Method. Soon after I marketed the book online, it became a bestseller on Amazon. After that, I focused on leveraging the book and started giving it away for free everywhere I could. I did many talks and events where I was able to gift my book to the audience, and through that activity, I began to build my readership and increase potential future customers even more. I even advertised so that people could land on my funnel, get my book for free, and then purchase a $47 product (my Writer's Success Toolkit, featuring a video course, workbook, and audio guide bundled together) if they wanted to go deeper and learn more from me. Once they bought this, they stayed on my email list, and I engaged with them every month for various free master classes, virtual events, and writing workshops.

The year I gave away about five thousand books, I got something back. I made over $250,000 in revenue in my business. It was the most I'd ever earned, and it's only increased since then as, over the last handful of years, I've built a very successful business doing the work I love and enjoy. This was possible because I leveraged my book instead of only trying to sell it. Of course I sold it initially, but once it became a bestseller, I decided it was time to start leveraging it. I then created assets for my ideal readers to buy and gave the book away for free everywhere I could and even taught the content in seminars and master classes. That was my engine. So you see, the PAE System was clearly at work here as I leveraged the book into substantial profit.

CASE STUDY: FROM $0 TO $100,000 IN 1 DAY

My author student Brandon did the same thing when he learned the PAE System and leveraged his book to create multiple six figures in revenue in his own business. One day, he called me up and told me that he had decided to give away a bunch of copies to one of his big prospects who was considering hiring him, as well as several others in the industry. He sent them fancy boxes with a signed copy of his book inside and a handwritten note. Later that day, when the books arrived, the prospect called him up delighted. He was so impressed by the book and everything Brandon had shared that he hired him on the spot, cutting a six-figure check. Talk about amazing, right?

Brandon has since repeated this effort and also started a podcast and other marketing efforts that have helped him create multiple six figures of revenue from his book alone.

CASE STUDY: DOUBLED PRICES

Before her book came out, my author student Cindy got clear on her assets, which were her coaching programs for women in midlife. She then decided to increase her prices after I encouraged her to double them. She also began selling private coaching packages at nearly double her previous rate. "I feel great," she told me. "Not only are my services in demand, but I'm finally charging what I'm worth. I've been doing this for thirty years and was never able to charge these prices. With the book and using the PAE System, I did it in just a few days."

The power of the PAE System is understanding how to focus on leveraging your book and not just selling it. Your book is worth more given away for free than it is sold because it acts as a sales and marketing tool that works for you, nonstop, as it makes its way from reader to reader. When you give your book away and begin leveraging it, you build reciprocity, authority or credibility, social proof, urgency, and commitment/consistency in the minds of your ideal readers. All of these are persuasive techniques that are key to generating sales and making money from your book now and forevermore. That's why a book is still the single best tool to leverage, and everyone who desires more credibility, authority, and impact should invest their time and resources in creating a high-quality book. I believe everyone who desires more income, impact, and an audience should have a book that can bring them additional revenue opportunities and the chance to earn more for themselves and their families. Everyone should be able to benefit from this system!

Sadly, not everyone is willing to venture further and learn what you have learned here today. Many people count themselves out before they try. They believe they could never write the book, let alone publish it, become a bestseller, and make any money from it. Don't let these people sway you to their way of thinking! Believe in yourself and your own potential. Wherever you lack skills, you can build them by reading books like this one, going to seminars, taking courses, and joining programs like Book Accelerator®. A great place to start that journey is right where you are. From here, you can explore the full suite of free offerings in the reader resources section of my website, which I've put together to help you reach your next level. Visit *www.writingcoachla.com/thecode* to access that for free at any time.

As you move forward in your journey, know that you can have everything you desire and create all the abundance, freedom, and happiness your heart longs for when you embrace these principles and put them into practice for yourself. You are reading these words because you know a book is in your future and you know you are supposed to become a successful author in your lifetime. So now is the time to finally commit to creating the book that you know is going to change your life and change you forever.

No author student who has been through my programs ever emerges as the same person. Everyone experiences a change, an awakening. We call this the *process of becoming* because there is so much potential for transformation when you commit and decide to write your book and become an author. As long as you are willing to put in the time and effort to learn and grow, there is nothing you cannot do! I always say I present the tools, the path, and the way, but you, the writer, must take the first step. You must walk that path. I can guide you, but I cannot move your feet for you. You must be a willing traveler.

So, I ask you now: Are you willing? Do you see the path spread out before you better than you did before reading this book? Do you believe you can have everything you desire and become a successful author? Because mastering all of this starts with that self-belief. It starts with the inner knowing that must be listened to. It starts with forming the undeniable inner compass to lead you where you must be led. Mastering the secrets of this book begins when you go forth and take the first step yourself.

When you do, everything you desire (writing your book, getting published, becoming a bestselling author, and making money from the things you love doing most) becomes possible. This is powerful work. You, the book, and the money you create will become powerful forces in the world. You will become an instrument of change and impact whether you know it or not. Having more visibility, more readers, more influence, and more profit allows you to continue the cycle and put more good back into the world, one new book at a time.

This is why the profitable author is a force to be reckoned with and an instrument of both impact and global change. What does that mean precisely, and how can you take your authorship and everything you create in this world to the next level? Read on to find out.

ACCESS THE CODE: AUTHOR MARKETING PLAYBOOK

If you'd like more advanced author marketing support, download my Author Marketing Playbook PDF from the reader resources section of my website at **www.writingcoachla.com/thecode.**

L.A. PERKINS

Ashley demystified writing and publishing a book! Both were not nearly as difficult as I had always assumed they would be, and that's because I followed Ashley's TAP Method for writing and then joined her Bestseller Legacy publishing program to get my book out into the world. The whole process has been truly empowering!

My book became an overnight #1 national bestseller on multiple retailer websites and sold over 4,000 copies within the first 2 months of its release. I also received a gold medal award from the Florida Authors and Publishers Association in the business/technology category.

Both during and since completing the programs, I've met so many wonderful new people and had conversations that would not otherwise occur, resulting in new clients and referrals and people approaching me with opportunities to be a guest speaker on shows and at events. In fact, since launching my book, the number of leads coming into my business has doubled! My bestselling book elevates me as a seasoned attorney in my area of practice, and the whole process has helped me hone my messaging and connect with my audiences like never before.

This is only the beginning! I cannot wait to see where my book takes me and my business next. But most importantly, I'm so thrilled to continue witnessing how it has helped other business owners avoid costly mistakes and protect the things that matter most.

—L.A. PERKINS, top-rated intellectual property attorney and bestselling author of *Why Brand Protection Matters*

BECOME A MASTER OF IMPACT

CHAPTER EIGHTEEN

THE 8TH SECRET

Become a Master of Impact

O N DECEMBER 19, 1843, a well-known author published a book that single-handedly changed the modern world forever.[18] That man was Charles Dickens, and the book was *A Christmas Carol*. The book wasn't his first, but it was the first of its kind. It was a little story about Christmas that would change the way people in the Western world would celebrate the holiday for centuries to come.

At first, Dickens had a hard time getting the book published because of the commercial failure of one of his other titles. His publishers didn't want his little Christmas book. They didn't quite understand his vision. It was a very distressing time for Dickens because he desperately needed money and for the book to be a hit. The only problem was no one would have it.

At the time, Christmas wasn't known as a big holiday. Many people today are shocked by this fact, but it's true. Christmas was a sleepy little nothing holiday. No big shopping experiences, no décor, feasts, or festive treats. It was all very ho-hum, in the way Easter or St. Patrick's Day can be for some. Yes, back then there was no commercial, big, loud, fanciful, crazy Christmas. Until, that is, Dickens wrote his book.

It wasn't until Dickens found the money himself and went to print that everything changed. He was able to get the book printed and even had a hand in designing the cover. It was a strange time because, frankly, no one but Dickens really understood his vision. But he persisted. He found the funds to make his book a reality. He hired the right people to help him, and soon the book was out there in the world before Christmastime. Remember, it wasn't a big holiday, but something shifted in 1843, when the book first came out. Slowly but surely, people began to read the book and share the story, and the world changed forever.

Did you know our entire idea of Christmas spirit—the feasts, the abundance, the celebration, and decorations—that we obsess over today began with that story, that book? Did you know that before, no one thought much of Christmas and today's levels of giving, celebrating, shopping, and eating simply weren't a part of it? But Dickens did something tremendous with his little story about Ebenezer Scrooge. Not only did he create a character that would become part of Christmas celebrations for millennia to come in hundreds if not thousands of films, television shows, books, and stage reincarnations, but he also changed the way the Western world saw and celebrated this religious holiday forever. Dickens changed culture, and he changed the world. He created the vision of modern Christmas we celebrate today in all its excess, abundance, and commercialism. And all of that started with a book, a book that has never been out of print since.

How would you like to be like Charles Dickens? To write something that has an impact so far-reaching that it stands the test of time and outlives you, your children, and your grandchildren? How would it feel to know that something you've written has had global impact and created global change? Is there something you care about deeply that you would like to get out there in a really big way? Perhaps you have a message or a story like Dickens's *A Christmas Carol* that needs to be heard. The good news is anyone can create a book that can change the world.

How is this possible? Have you ever read a book that changed your world? I'm sure you have! To me, each book is a window into the author's mind and way of thinking, their way of seeing things. Books change lives by opening our minds to those different worlds, whether fiction or nonfiction. Both types of books can have this impact. Here are more examples of both fiction and nonfiction books that have changed the world and had a lasting impact.

FAHRENHEIT 451 BY RAY BRADBURY

In the late 1940s, Ray Bradbury wrote a novel entitled *Fahrenheit 451*. It was a book that took him several attempts to write, beginning first as a series of short stories that then became a novella. It was published in October 1953 by the Ballantine Publishing Group. *Fahrenheit 451* tells a rather dark story about the future, where humanity is deeply depressed, addicted to the oversized screens in their houses, and unable to function without them. There are rules, too, in this horrible demagoguery of the future. Books have all been erased from existence, and a swath of guards with the power to burn them one by one rule the cities, serving the government. It's a frightening image of humanity without books, stories, and reading. Bradbury depicts humans as depressed, pill-addicted, and suicidal because of the screens and the lack of books in the world. Do you think he may have been onto something?

In fact, because his book so pointedly describes humanity and this dark, desolate future, the novel was censored and even banned multiple times from the 1950s to the early 2000s. Despite this, the book remains a classic work of American literature. Like Dickens's *A Christmas Carol*, *Fahrenheit 451* has never been out of print and has sold over ten million copies since it was first published.[19] Bradbury's enduring legacy no doubt stems from his chief aim in writing the book to be "a *preventer* of futures, not a predictor of them."[20] Everything he wrote about in his novel was designed to prevent the atrocities he imagined.

Books have the power to change the world because they have the power to change us. They reach into our souls, our minds, our hearts. They make us think, and they make us question. The book is one of the most powerful forms of human creation, in my opinion, because of its transformative power. From author to text, to reader, and to author again, the cycle is one that can have a ripple effect beyond words. There are books that have healed humanity, books that have changed culture, books that have upended the status quo, and books that have brought to light elements of our shared experience so we may know that we are ultimately not alone, that there is purpose in our pain, and that a greater, higher power connects us all and all that is.

THE DIARY OF A YOUNG GIRL BY ANNE FRANK

I first read the diary of Anne Frank in school, and then I read it again as an adult. The first time I read it, I thought I was reading fiction and didn't understand that the beautiful and terrible events of this narrator's life actually happened. Her voice—so intelligent, so pure and powerful, so full of light and hope—was beyond anything I'd ever read before. It seemed impossible to grasp that this young girl was only thirteen years old at the time of writing in Nazi Germany. Anne Frank detailed her life and her terribly difficult childhood growing up in hiding inside the secret annex of a building Otto Frank used for his businesses with finesse and imagination. The miracle of the book is not merely that it survived but that it transports readers back to a place and time that most of us learn about through history books but can never really know. Her book helps us understand these events to the extent that we can and serves as a powerful reminder of what happened to Jews and their families during World War II, now distant and becoming even more so for many young people today. Many books have fictionalized the experience of war and genocide, but Anne Frank brought it to us through her own personal account, which has become one of the most well-known and widely adapted and translated books in the world for this reason.

INSTRUMENTS OF GLOBAL CHANGE

As we've seen, books are instruments of global change because they have the power to change us. The transference of knowledge, of story, of experience from one person to another can only happen in this specific way through a book. Books hold a special power to move us and persuade us. The book has persuasive power because there is a connection that is made between the reader and the writer through things like tone, structure, voice, evidence, argument, and story.

Stories themselves are highly persuasive. Stories have been shown to be twenty-two times more memorable than facts alone[21] Therefore, when your entire book is structured like one big, powerful narrative story, it too holds miraculous persuasive power. Think of a good book in your life that has forever changed you. Were you not a different person when you started the book than when you finished it? Of course! Books truly change our minds, our hearts, and our beliefs. They challenge and provoke us. They stir our thoughts and make us question our perception of reality, our biases, our norms, and our behaviors.

Books can be powerful, amazing tools that can be used to sow seeds of light and goodness in the world or to sow seeds of hate, misery, and war. In 1925, a man in a prison cell sat down and wrote a book detailing his hatred and antisemitism. He was a troubled man who'd led a troubled life. He wanted to be an actor but had failed at it many times. Instead, he went on to become a writer, spinning tales and creating speeches in the political arena. That book was *Mein Kampf,* and the man was Adolf Hitler. Hitler wrote the book, and his hateful philosophies spread like wildfire. Many people assumed that because he could write and deliver his message through words, he was someone to be listened to, someone to be revered. His messages and hateful philosophies became the basis of a mass genocide and the reason the world went to war twice that century, as well as the reason millions of Jews were systematically murdered.[22]

So you see, books have the power to ignite good in the world but also great evil. As you read on, I hope you will anchor your good intentions. I hope you will think about how your book can spread a message of love, peace, acceptance, positivity, goodness, and light. We need to use books for what they were created to be—our collective healing, our salvation, our gateway to a better world.

So how do we ensure our books are able to fulfill this? How do we ensure they can change minds and change the world for the better? I don't have all the answers, but what I do know is that this very book you are reading is part of my mission to do the same thing—to create powerful change through my words, no matter how large or how small, and to empower aspiring authors to do the same when they learn to write and publish books that put goodness back into the world.

My mission is to help aspiring authors who are struggling with their books to have an easier, faster, better time getting them out and into the world. I want you and everyone you encounter to read this book and know that if you are someone who desires to tell your story or share your message, you should write your book in order to help others and make the world a better place, and it doesn't have to be difficult or feel impossible to do so. You don't have to wait until late in life or rent a cabin in the woods for a year. You don't need to put a stop to your business and everything else you are doing. You can do this now! Really! With this book, my chief aim is to transfer my beliefs, my knowledge, and my experience to you so you can forever shift the way you think about writing and publishing books. My goal by doing so is to impact many readers through this book and build a community of people who believe in the transformative power of books.

What is your vision? I encourage you now to go back to your *why* and consider the message you are putting into the world through your book. What is it, and why does it matter? Once you have that message clear in your mind, write it down and begin sharing it with others. Continue doing so as you move through the writing and publishing process and never lose sight of your message and its importance. Hold fast to your vision, for the world needs to hear what you have to say.

ACCESS THE CODE: CREATE A BOOK OF IMPACT

To get my four-part formula for creating a book of impact, download my SLIC Framework PDF from the reader resources section of my website at ***www.writingcoachla.com/thecode.***

Author Success Story
NATALIE GLEBOVA

I followed Ashley's TAP Method to write my second book, so I wasn't new to the process of writing, but her program was still so incredibly eye-opening and rewarding. Since my book touches on the subject of transformation, spiritual death and rebirth, new beginnings, and healing old patterns, I lived this process as I was writing the book, which aligned so amazingly with the mindset practices of the TAP Method.

After completing my manuscript in less than 90 days, then joining Ashley's Publishing Master program to prepare to pitch my book to traditional publishers, I ended up signing with my dream publisher. Since it's been published, I've gotten more opportunities to speak at universities and have appeared on several podcasts, most notably popular self-improvement podcasts that have tens of millions of total downloads. It's been a great opportunity to gather more followers and grow my community.

But the most important change for me as a result of writing and publishing my book has been an internal one. I have found my freedom, reclaimed my voice to speak my truth, and discovered my power to stand on my own without being emotionally dependent on anyone. The changes I've witnessed in myself have really been incredible.

Now, I have plans to rebuild my coaching business bigger and better than ever, thanks to the success of my book and my new-found ability to live with an open heart. Remember: everything in life happens for us, not to us. I believe this even more fiercely after having taken part in Ashley's programs and embracing all that has come my way as a result.

This journey has been incredible, and I now feel I'm contributing to the world more, which means I'm bringing more value to more people and, ultimately, to my work itself. And my publisher feels the same way, because I soon have a second book coming out! This journey has changed my life in so many ways I never thought possible.

—Natalie Glebova, bestselling author of Temple of Love

Author Success Story
PAM AUGUST

I had been told for years that I needed to write a book, that the world needed to hear the "Pamisms" my life's work had led me to collect and develop. But I wasn't ready to write a book or "be an author." I kept switching between believing I was a person of impact and that I was merely an imposter. Who did I think I was to be writing a book? That question kept holding me back.

Until I met Ashley.

Right from our first conversation, her belief in me and what I had to share carried me through my initial doubts and the rewarding yet intense, strategic, and creative journey of my initial manuscript—which I completed in less than eight weeks! Her team's expert support and guidance also took my book through editing and created a publishing proposal that landed me not one but three publishing offers!

Not only do I now have a book out in the world which I am so proud of as a concrete expression of what I offer others, but I now own the identity of "author." This shift has transformed my business and my life.

And the journey was so much easier than I thought it would be. At some point in the process, it was like I stopped writing my book and it started writing me. The process made me a clearer and more confident person who was more compelling both on and off the page. My book has positioned me as a thought leader in my field, resulting in higher-value client engagements, more speaking opportunities, and global impact as I am sought after by organizations around the world. It has truly created the foundation for my next evolution.

—PAM AUGUST, bestselling author of *Potential*

Go Further Faster with a Mentor and Expert Guide

CHAPTER NINETEEN

THE 9TH SECRET

Go Further Faster with a Mentor and Expert Guide

NOW THAT YOU'VE LEARNED these many secrets, the question is are you ready to get your book out there and be the successful author you know you're destined to be? Are you ready to become a global change agent with the power of your book in the world? There is one secret left, and it is especially important because it will inform your very first step in the journey of writing your book and becoming an author. The ninth secret is the mentor secret, because I encourage you to get help and avoid walking this path alone.

If you're at all like the way I used to be, the thought of asking for help from someone makes you cringe. When I first started out, I didn't understand the mentor secret, and I didn't ask anyone for help. I mistakenly believed I needed to succeed on my own and that everyone who had accomplished something great did so without help or guidance. I think this misconception was perpetuated by seeing so many of the great minds and artists working alone, in isolation. We have this misconception in our society—the perception of the sole, mad genius. We picture Albert Einstein, Frida Kahlo, Benjamin Franklin, Toni Morrison, Marie Curie, Langston Hughes, William Shakespeare, Nelson Mandela, Virginia Woolf, Ernest Hemingway, Nikola Tesla, and others madly at work alone in their offices or laboratories. We see them isolated from society and consumed by their solo endeavors. But it's a mistake to view them as solopreneurs, because the truth is anyone who goes far in this life does so with help, community, and support.

Now, this is not to say your own self-mastery, your own work ethic, isn't important. It is! This book has been all about self-mastery, after all. From your *why* to your big idea, to finding and serving your ideal readers, to believing you can become a bestselling and profitable author. I am all for developing mastery of the self. That process of development, however, almost never happens in isolation. It happens with guidance, with a mentor, with someone who has been where you are trying to go, and often with a community of people around you. They say it takes a village to raise a child, but it also takes a village to write and publish a good book and become an author. If you check the acknowledgments section of any book, you will see for yourself: there is a whole army of people to thank because the author had a whole army of support.

It is wise to start building your army now. You will need all types of people and all different areas of expertise to help and guide you. But let's start with this first step: getting a mentor.

YOUR MENTOR IS YOUR PATH TO SUCCESS

What is a mentor anyway? A mentor is an experienced and trusted advisor, someone who can guide someone younger or with less experience toward their goals successfully. I have had many mentors in my life who did this for me, even from a young age. In college, I had many professors who inspired and encouraged me, and one in particular whom I found when I decided to take a graduate-level writing class.

Getting into this class was one of the hardest and most rewarding things I'd ever done. I had some confidence in my writing but never truly knew whether I was any good, even though some people had said I was a good writer growing up. I felt I needed proof—and a lot more training. So there I was, a sophomore, trying to weasel my way into a graduate-level creative writing course called "The Art of the Short Story" taught by Professor Chuck Rosenthal. I sent several emails trying to beg my way in, to no avail, and finally decided to simply send a story I'd written instead. I cannot remember what I sent, only that it was mostly pretty awful but something I felt the slightest tinge of pride in. I think I phrased the accompanying email as something like "Please give me a shot and I promise I will work hard and learn everything. If I suck, you can kick me out of your class."

The email I got back was a one-liner, something to the tune of, "Okay, you're in. Try to keep up."

I was elated! After all, Chuck Rosenthal was *the* professor you went to at Loyola Marymount University if you wanted to learn creative writing. He was the man. Everyone told tales about how he was so creative and had so much success with his books. There were rumors of red wine and crazy stories flying around his classroom—both of which proved to be true. There was a reason it was a graduate-level class—because everyone was older and more experienced. But at this stage, that didn't matter. I only needed two things: more knowledge and someone to believe in me.

I wrote *a lot* in the course—more than I ever had before. Some of it was decent, some of it was plain awful, and I still cringe today thinking of a few of my stories. But some of my writing was actually pretty good, and Rosenthal believed in me. After a while, he wasn't shy about telling me so—and telling everyone else too. On the last day of class, he held up my short story after reading the entire thing out loud (much to my embarrassment). At the end, he looked up at the class, waved my manuscript, and shouted emphatically, "Now *that* is a story!"

Rosenthal gave me good advice about my writing and told me to keep at it. He knew that I could "do this," meaning write and be published. It was a well-known fact that most people didn't hear this from him and that he would actively dissuade many people from pursuing a writing career. Everyone talked about how he was unusually harsh and unflinching with his grading and how most people didn't do so well in his class. But that was never my experience. Rosenthal was the perfect mentor for me because his perceived tough grading and opinionated style of teaching not only helped me build valuable skills but allowed me to test my own limits, challenge myself, and form both courage and self-belief. His teachings and mentorship have stayed with me to this day, and I count myself lucky to not only have had him as my professor multiple times but to have been let into that graduate-level course long ago.

Rosenthal set something in motion in me, and soon I found other mentors in my life who would push me toward my goals and help me realize my potential. We all need mentors to support and guide us, to help us recognize and realize our potential. As an aspiring author, you need someone to believe in you as well as a hand to guide you lovingly yet firmly toward your goals. Today, I have many mentors, so many that I've lost count! I seek counsel from everyone—my team, other talented and successful authors, coaches, business owners, leaders in organizations I admire, and others who have been where I want to go. I have spent around $250,000 hiring mentors in the last few years so that I could learn from them and improve myself, my mindset, my skills, and my business in the process. I have business mentors, writing and publishing mentors, marketing mentors, mindset mentors, and more.

So, where do you find a mentor to help you get your book out there? The most obvious answer is to look where you want to go and see who is already enjoying the destination. You can also look for a mentor who has guided others in the same direction and who is good at giving advice to a particular type of person. What do I mean by this? Well, for example, I am a mentor and a coach for first-time authors specifically. Seasoned authors usually don't come to me because, often, they have already mastered many of the things I teach. But first-time authors have a unique experience, one that I believe I am perfectly suited to help them with because of my own experiences.

This is why I have devoted my business and my work to helping people who are writing their very first book and are dedicated to the process of becoming a successful author in the world. This is a very unique type of person, mind you. You know this, because if you are reading this book, you most likely *are* this person. You know you have many fears, challenges, hopes, and dreams. You also know deep down that you are meant for more, that you are meant to do this work in the world. You desire the credibility, the validation, the respect, and yes, maybe even the fame and fortune too. But the thing that really drives you, the thing that keeps you up at night, is the notion of exploring your full potential. You want to see if you really have it in you to succeed. You want to know if you can make it to the 1 percent, the percentage of people who actually become successful authors and go on to have amazing lives and careers doing what they love and helping people in the process.

My role is to help you make it into the 1 percent and to see this number grow and grow so that as many people as possible can access this level of success for themselves. I believe everyone who wants to write and publish should be able to and should have immense success with their books. To me, this isn't a great expectation to remain unfulfilled; it's simply the way I believe that God—the Universe, life, greater intelligence—knows that we must go as humans. Gone are the days of authorship being an elitist pursuit, closed off to the masses. Gone are the days when women, people of color, and those disenfranchised and marginalized by society do not have voices. This is a very different world from 1440, the year the printing press was first invented. Johannes Gutenberg would not have believed the way books have exploded throughout our society. And yet, maybe that's exactly what he would believe, because that's exactly what he saw when he invented it. Perhaps that was always his vision.

WAYS TO GET HELP

First off, you have one of the best ways to get help right here in your hands. Read books like this one—and a lot of them. Seek out the mentors—the authors—who wrote those books, find more opportunities to work with them, and get their support. For example, by the time you finish reading this book, you will have a whole bunch of information on my programs and offerings, as well as access to the free reader resources section on my website at *www.writingcoachla.com/thecode*. I've made sure to share this multiple times so you know how easy it is to get help when you need it. I wish I'd had that level of help and support when I first started, but I am glad to know you won't have to struggle the way I did to become the author you know you are destined to be. It's my goal to make this next step as easy for you as possible, which is why I've created resources that are free and resources and solutions at various investment levels. There is something for every single person who reads this book, and I have no doubt there is something for you too.

Make no mistake, this is the way. You must seek out the right education and guidance from experts. You must be open-minded and willing to grow. You must be coachable and willing to learn. You must trust those who have come before you and not try to reinvent the wheel. Model what works and you will achieve success. If you merely try to make it on your own, as I once did, you will have a long and arduous road ahead of you. Trust in those who have already cleared and walked the path many times. Trust those who know the journey like the back of their hand. Listen to those who understand the emotional side and can guide you fully and properly. Take advice from those who have stepped into the potholes themselves, who know the pitfalls and can help you save time and make fewer mistakes than they did. This is the way.

When you open yourself up to finding your mentor, you will realize potential mentors are all around you. As the saying goes, when the student is ready, the teacher will appear. Grant yourself the opportunity to find your teacher and trust in someone who has already helped others reach their goals. Give your hopes, dreams, aspirations, and fears to them so they can hold these for a little while. Let yourself be taught, guided, steered, believed in, and supported in your relationship with this person.

One important thing to note about mentorship: this person has to want for you what they want for themselves and more. That is, they have to be 100 percent in your corner, rooting for your highest degree of success. Be wary of mentors who are intimidated by you or your goals, who shoot you down, who unnecessarily critique you or try to put you off your chosen path because they believe it's too ambitious. Be wary of those who feel that by succeeding, you are somehow taking away from their success. If you find one of these people, run for the hills! You need not waste time with those who don't fully support you, back you, and 100 percent root for you.

I have no doubt you will find many mentors in your lifetime, should you only begin to look for them and seek them out. The point is not to find a single mentor but a mentor who can help you in your journey based on where you are right now. Who is that person? I know that if you only open yourself to finding them, they will appear, and it will be your time.

IT ALL STARTS WITH YOU

Remember that wherever you wish to go on this journey of writing your book and becoming the author you were meant to be in this world, it all starts with you. I once heard a well-known businessman talk about the notion that our ideas are not ours but divinely gifted. God places these gifts in our hearts for a reason, so we may be good shepherds of the ideas within us, and we must all be good shepherds. This applies to you and your book as well. Be a good shepherd of your book idea. Look after it. Nurture it with learning, with careful study of those who have already succeeded in accomplishing their dreams, and with a mentor who can properly guide you and hold the belief for you when you need it most, then give it back to you when you are ready. The first step is always to decide and take action.

Books can change the world. You know this deep down because books have changed *your* world. Perhaps reading this book has been the change you needed, the inspiration, the motivation, the information required to get you from where you are, with idea and impulse, to where you want to be: a decisive action taker and someone who will not only write their book but see it through to publication and monetization too.

Throughout this book, we have covered the 9 most powerful untold secrets that will help you succeed in your authorship and build the life and career you dream of. They are secret because they might be common practice in some circles but certainly not common knowledge. Now, they can be both for you. It's my hope that you will use these 9 secrets to better your life and improve the quality and experience of writing your first book and every single book you write thereafter. I hope you will use these teachings to mold yourself into the author you are meant to be and put good back into the world through your books.

If I could encourage you to do one thing, it would be to take action once you finish the last page of this book, close it, and set it down. Do something with what you've read. Whether you come to me and seek out support from my company or another, I don't care. What I do care about is that you do something with what you read and stop letting time drift by while your book idea sits within you, begging you to do something with it. It's so important now more than ever that you take action. Remember that tomorrow isn't promised to us. There is no guarantee that you will wake up tomorrow as you are today and be able to fulfill your dreams. Do what you can while you can, and the rest will take care of itself.

Most of all, remember your deepest *why* and your reason for your desires. Remember the reason you decided to do this in the first place. Remember your ideal reader who needs you. For moments of great challenge and difficulty, one of the most helpful things I ever heard was from one of my authors, who also happens to be one of my mentors. She said, "You have to get beyond yourself. That's the only thing to do."[23] And she was right.

You must find a way to get beyond yourself with this book. Because in the end, it isn't about you. Even though the content may move through you, it is about much more than you. It is about the lives and the readers you will impact. It is about the legacy you will leave. It is about your family and friends who will benefit from your success and your ability to pursue and achieve your dreams. It is about others who will look to you as a source of inspiration when you accomplish the great things you are meant for in this life. It is about the lives you will impact as you come full circle and become a mentor to those who are just beginning. I want that for you and so much more.

Now is your time to go and find the mentor who can take you where you want to go. I cannot wait for you to succeed! I can't wait to be standing in line at your book signing. To open *The New York Times Book Review* and see your name on the bestsellers list. To open my email and hear about the one million copies of your book sold worldwide. To see you speak on stages and land that TED Talk. To hear about the awards and accolades you've been given for the impact you have had. To watch the ripple effect that occurs from the global change you have started with your book.

Thank you for being here. Thank you for reading these words. Thank you for entrusting me with your time and your journey of authorship. Now take the next step and do what you know you must. In case you haven't noticed, I have been your mentor for a short while in these pages. It's my hope that I can continue to be your mentor in times to come, but for now, I will do what all good mentors must do and transfer my belief in you back to you so that you can own it, hold it, magnify it, and watch it grow. Now is your time, dear reader. And I cannot *wait* to see what you create!

Author Success Story
WHITNEY LYN ALLEN

Ashley and her team were incredibly instrumental in me finally publishing not one but two books. I had a bold goal of writing and publishing a book that would help other people going through grief and trauma by connecting with my own story. But I was incredibly overwhelmed and didn't know how to get started or what to do because there is so much that goes into the publishing process that many people don't realize.

Ashley and her team took my rough manuscript through each step of the publishing processes of editing, cover design, and even marketing to not only make my book the best it could be but help me achieve my goal of getting it out into the world and making it a bestseller. And it all happened in less than six months.

Many people have ideas for books that could help so many people, but self-publishing without someone who knows the market and how to make your book a product that people actually want to read and how to get it in front of the right eyes is the hard part. Ashley and her team take the guesswork out of publishing so your ideas and teachings can come to life.

For my second book, I decided that I wanted to give traditional publishing a try to make the process even more hands-off for me as I became busier with how my first book was still helping grow my business. And Ashley and her team were still the first people I thought of to help me prepare for that process. I knew that getting a book traditionally published in today's market is very competitive and difficult, so I wanted guidance in writing a strong manuscript and querying it to literary agents and publishers for the best possible chance to publish with a traditional publisher.

With Ashley and her team's help, my book was presented to the market in the best possible light, and I was able to secure a traditional publishing deal with an advance amount offered that has become incredibly rare to see in the traditional market these days. I truly don't believe that would have been possible without not only the expertise and guidance from Ashley's team but also the success they guided me to in self-publishing my first book and the sales history and notoriety that provided. I am so thankful to them and so excited for what the future holds.

—WHITNEY LYN Allen, bestselling author of *Running in Trauma Stilettos* and *What Must Be Carried*

The Author Within You Awaits

NOW THAT YOU'VE FINISHED reading this book, you may be wondering, *What's next?*

The author within you awaits! It's time to embrace your inner author and begin the journey. Now that you know better, you can *do* better and finally take the leap for yourself. I have created a range of free reader resources you can access right now to help you get started. You can find all of the items mentioned in this book and so much more at *www.writingcoachla.com/thecode*.

HOW TO GET MORE SUPPORT FROM US

My company offers a range of options to get further coaching, mentorship, and support. I've shared some options with you already, but to learn more, visit writingcoachla.com and find out about the programs and courses we currently have to offer.

With that said, here are two ways to get started writing your book with me and my team:

1. Join my free 5-Day "Get Your Book Done" Boot camp!
   This is a high-energy, exclusive, virtual event that we run throughout the year to help you write a book that will unlock doors and grow your audience, impact, and income this year. Register for free by scanning the QR code below:

2. Join Book Accelerator®, my 90-day book writing program!
   This is a high-touch, three-month coaching program taught by myself and other industry experts who have collectively helped over a thousand authors reach their full potential. We open up a few spots in Book Accelerator® throughout the year. Apply for Book Accelerator® by scanning the QR code below:

I encourage you to take action on one of the two options right now. Don't wait! We are here to help and guide you on your journey. Now is your time! You got this!

HELP ME SPREAD THE WORD

If you enjoyed this book and it has been helpful to you, please do me a favor and let others know about it. Share it online, leave a review on the platform or site that you bought it from, and tell your friends, family, and network about it.

When you post about this book online, remember to tag me so I can see it and say thank you. I have also been known to send readers thank-you gifts and fun surprises when they share my work, so please don't be surprised if you hear from me personally when you tag me in one of your posts and share this book!

Remember, a book holds tremendous power to change lives and the world, one reader at a time, so if this book has helped you, be that change for someone who needs it and help them by gifting them a copy or loaning yours instead.

SHARE YOUR THOUGHTS AND FEEDBACK

What did you think of this book? Has *The Author's Success Code* changed the game for you and made an impact? If so, I'd love to hear about it! Send me an email and let me know what the most impactful part of the book was and how it has helped you on your journey. I genuinely would love to hear from you! You can email me at *ashley@writingcoachla.com*.

THANK YOU AND A BONUS GIFT!

Thank you for reading this book. If you've gotten to this page, I want you to know you are awesome and deserve a little something extra. That's why I would love to gift you something really exciting. Visit my website and you will get a special thank-you gift from me, including a bonus of one of the lost chapters of this book. You can claim your free gift now at *www.writingcoachla.com/gift*.

Acknowledgments

I AM EXCEPTIONALLY grateful to my amazing team at LA Writing Coach and Brands Through Books for their ongoing support, dedication, and willingness to join me and be part of our collective effort to help aspiring authors create amazing, life-changing books. Without them, I wouldn't be able to do the work I love so much and serve and support so many aspiring authors. I owe a special thanks to my editor, Melody, for her insightful comments, her guidance on what was needed most in this book, and her help with enhancing that message. I also owe special thanks to my lead coach and team member Jess for taking the time to help me navigate the complex world of publishing for myself and for being a positive enthusiast and proponent of everything we teach our authors. Thank you to my team lead, Chelsea, for her consistency, dedication, and incredible follow-through not just on this very book publication project but for all our authors as well.

Thank you to all our authors and students who allowed me to feature them in this book and who willingly shared their stories and successes for our readers. Of course, I am deeply humbled and grateful to them all for allowing me to guide them on their journeys to becoming authors for the first time and entrusting me and my team with their stories and messages. Because of them, I wake up every day excited to venture into the world of book writing and publishing, grateful that I can spend my "work" days doing something I deeply love and care about.

I also want to thank my family for supporting me in my own journey to becoming an author and business owner. The two efforts are surprisingly similar in the qualities they require and the demands they place upon your time. My family has been there for the early mornings, the late nights, and the days in between that seem to be long stretches of time spent dedicated to the work of being an author, coach, and business owner. Thank you to my husband, Craig, for your steadfastness, your willingness to support my wildest goals and dreams, and for always letting me know how loved I am. Thank you to my mom for being a rock in my life and being there in the times I needed you most. To my beautiful daughter, Bella—you are and will always be the greatest love of my life, and I can't wait until you can write your own success story someday!

It goes without saying that I could not do this work alone, and I wouldn't want to try. Writing and publishing books—and owning a business dedicated to the like—takes a village. I am so incredibly grateful, humbled, and overflowing with appreciation for mine.

End Notes

1   "Analysis: Study Says 81 Percent of Americans Say They Could Write a Book [DP]," Morning Edition, October 21, 2002, *link.gale.com/apps/doc/ A162251218/AONE?u=anon~5d6492ad&sid=sitemap&xid=5e2e7dc6*; Leilanie Stewart, "How Many People Who Write a Novel Finish It and How Many Get Published?" leilaniestewart.com, March 16, 2022, *leilaniestewart.com/2022/03/16/how-many-people-who-write-a-novel- finish-it-and-how-many-get-published/*

2   Joseph Epstein, "Think You Have a Book in You? Think Again," *The New York Times,* September 28, 2002, *www.nytimes.com/2002/09/28/ opinion/think-you-have-a-book-in-you-think-again.html*

3   Epstein, "Think You Have a Book in You?"

4   The price of a high-quality book in 1400 is listed as being over £24. According to a historical conversion, this equates to a modern valuation of over $38,000 USD. Joanne Filippone Overty, "The Cost of Doing Scribal Business: Prices of Manuscript Books in England, 1300-1483," *Book History* 11 (2008): 5, *http://www.jstor.org/stable/30227411*; Eric W. Nye, "Pounds Sterling to Dollars: Historical Conversion of Currency," University of Wyoming, accessed November 17, 2024, *www.uwyo.edu/ numimage/currency.htm*

5 Yasmeen Turayhi, "How to Finally Finish Your Book," Medium, September 7, 2021, *yasmeenturayhi.medium.com/i-recently-learned-that-over-82-of-americans-want-to-write-a-book-but-less-than-1-of-americans-492cd5c900c8#:~:text=Socrates%20 said%20%E2%80%9CThe%20unexamined%20 life,enough%E2%80%9D%2C%20and%20how%20you%20react*

6 Epstein, "Think You Have a Book in You?"

7 Rob Errera, "How Many Books Are Published Each Year? [2024 Statistics]," Toner Buzz, August 18, 2023, *www.tonerbuzz.com/blog/ how-many-books-are-published-each-year/#:~:text=Figures%20 range%20from%20500%2C000%20to,book%20titles%20 published%20each%20year*

8 Rhea Hirshman, "Bookworms Live Longer," *Yale Alumni Magazine*, November/December 2016, *www.yalealumnimagazine.com/ articles/4377-bookworms-live-longer*

9 Heidi Moawad, "Benefits of Reading Books: How It Can Positively Affect Your Life," Healthline, October 15, 2019, *www.healthline. com/health/benefits-of-reading-books*; University of Cambridge, "Reading for Pleasure Early in Childhood Linked to Better Cognitive Performance and Mental Wellbeing in Adolescence," EurekAlert!, June 27, 2023, *www.eurekalert.org/news-releases/993270*

10 Napoleon Hill, *Think and Grow Rich* (The Ralston Society, 1937), 17.

11 Emiliana R. Simon-Thomas, "How Strong Is Your Sense of Purpose in Life?" *Greater Good Magazine*, April 11, 2022, *greatergood. berkeley.edu/article/item/how_strong_is_your_sense_of_purpose_ in_life#:~:text=According%20to%20research%2C%20having%20 purpose,have%20better%20health%20and%20longevity.*

12   *Merriam-Webster.com Dictionary,* s.v. "Author," accessed October 29, 2024, *www.merriam-webster.com/dictionary/author.*

13   Quoted in Duncan White, *Nabokov and His Books: Between Late Modernism and the Literary Marketplace* (Oxford University Press, 2017), 158.

14   *Merriam-Webster.com Dictionary,* s.v. "Impulse," accessed October 21, 2024, *www.merriam-webster.com/dictionary/impulse#:~:text=%3A%20 a%20sudden%20spontaneous%20inclination%20or%20incitement%20 to%20some%20usually%20unpremeditated%20action*

15   Shannon Hale (@haleshannon), "When writing a first draft, I have to remind myself constantly that I'm only shoveling sand into a box so later I can build castles," Twitter, August 27, 2015, *x.com/haleshannon/ status/636907891379736576?lang=en.*

16   Brendon Burchard, "What Is The Confidence-Competence Loop?" Facebook, March 11, 2021, *www.facebook.com/ watch/?v=517421122596174*

17   Jay Conrad Levinson et al., *Guerrilla Marketing for Writers: 100 No-Cost, Low-Cost Weapons for Selling Your Work,* expanded 2nd ed. (Morgan James Publishing, 2010).

18   Paulette Beete, "Ten Things to Know About Charles Dickens' *A Christmas Carol,*" National Endowment for the Arts, December 4, 2020, *www.arts.gov/stories/blog/2020/ten-things-know-about-charles-dickens-christmas-carol#:~:text=Story%20of%20Christmas.-,Did%20 you%20know%E2%80%A6,long%20nighttime%20walks%20 around%20London.*

19 "Fahrenheit 451," American Writers Museum, accessed October 24, 2024, *exhibits.americanwritersmuseum.org/exhibits/ ray-bradbury-inextinguishable/fahrenheit-451/*

20 Paraphrased from "Beyond 1984: The People Machines" (1979): "People ask me to predict the Future, when all I want to do is prevent it. Better yet, build it. Predicting [the future] is much too easy, anyway. You look at the people around you, the street you stand on, the visible air you breathe, and predict more of the same. To hell with more. I want better." Ray Bradbury, "Beyond 1984: The People Machines," in *Yestermorrow: Obvious Answers to Impossible Futures* (RosettaBooks, 2017), 126, Kindle.

21 Kate Harrison, "A Good Presentation Is About Data and Story," Forbes, January 20, 2015, *www.forbes.com/sites/ kateharrison/2015/01/20/a-good-presentation-is-about-data-and-story/*.

22 "Adolf Hitler Publishes 'Mein Kampf,'" Anne Frank House, accessed November 23, 2024, *www.annefrank.org/en/timeline/6/ adolf-hitler-publishes-mein-kampf/*.

23 Louise Seirmarco-Yale, *Art, You Be the Judge: Reawaken Your Instincts and Enjoy Art on Your Own Terms* (Seirmarco Art LLC, 2024).

BIBLIOGRAPHY

American Writers Museum. "Fahrenheit 451." October 24, 2024. *exhibits. americanwritersmuseum.org/exhibits/ray-bradbury-inextinguishable/ fahrenheit-451/.*

Anne Frank House. "Adolf Hitler Publishes 'Mein Kampf.'" Accessed November 23, 2024. *www.annefrank.org/en/timeline/6/ adolf-hitler-publishes-mein-kampf/.*

Beete, Paulette. "Ten Things to Know About Charles Dickens' *A Christmas Carol.*" National Endowment for the Arts. December 4, 2020. *www. arts.gov/stories/blog/2020/ten-things-know-about-charles-dickens-christmas-carol#:~:text=Story%20of%20Christmas.-,Did%20you%20 know%E2%80%A6,long%20nighttime%20walks%20around%20London.*

Bradbury, Ray. "Beyond 1984: The People Machines." In *Yestermorrow: Obvious Answers to Impossible Futures.* RosettaBooks, 2017. Kindle.

Burchard, Brendon. "What Is The Confidence-Competence Loop?" Facebook. March 11, 2021. *www.facebook.com/watch/?v=517421122596174.*

Epstein, Joseph. "Think You Have a Book in You? Think Again." *The New York Times.* September 28, 2002. *www.nytimes.com/2002/09/28/opinion/think-you-have-a-book-in-you-think-again.html.*

Errera, Rob. "How Many Books Are Published Each Year?" Toner Buzz. August 18, 2023. www.tonerbuzz.com/blog/how-many-books-are-published-each-year/#:~:text=Figures%20range%20from%20500%2C000%20to,book%20titles%20published%20each%20year.

Galaxy Press. "The Story Behind Fahrenheit 451." Accessed November 23, 2024. *galaxypress.com/story-behind-fahrenheit-451/.*

Harrison, Kate. "A Good Presentation Is About Data and Story." Forbes. January 20, 2015. www.forbes.com/sites/kateharrison/2015/01/20/a-good-presentation-is-about-data-and-story/.

Hill, Napoleon. *Think and Grow Rich. The Ralston Society, 1937.*

Hirshman, Rhea. "Bookworms Live Longer." *Yale Alumni Magazine.* November/December 2016. *www.yalealumnimagazine.com/articles/4377-bookworms-live-longer.*

Levinson, Jay Conrad, Rick Frishman, Michael Larsen, and David L. Hancock. *Guerrilla Marketing for Writers: 100 No-Cost, Low-Cost Weapons for Selling Your Work.* Expanded 2nd ed. Morgan James Publishing, 2010.

Moawad, Heidi. "Benefits of Reading Books: How It Can Positively Affect Your Life." Healthline. October 15, 2019. *www.healthline.com/health/benefits-of-reading-books.*

Morning Edition. "Analysis: Study Says 81 Percent of Americans Say They Could Write a Book [DP]." October 21, 2002. *link.gale.com/apps/doc/A162251218/AONE?u=anon~5d6492ad&sid=sitemap&xid=5e2e7dc6.*

Nye, Eric W. "Pounds Sterling to Dollars: Historical Conversion of Currency." University of Wyoming. Accessed November 17, 2024. *www.uwyo.edu/numimage/currency.htm.*

Overty, Joanne Filippone. "The Cost of Doing Scribal Business: Prices of Manuscript Books in England, 1300-1483." *Book History* 11 (2008): 1–32. http://www.jstor.org/stable/30227411.

Seirmarco-Yale, Louise. *Art, You Be the Judge: Reawaken Your Instincts and Enjoy Art on Your Own Terms.* Seirmarco Art LLC, 2024.

Simon-Thomas, Emiliana R. "How Strong Is Your Sense of Purpose in Life?" *Greater Good Magazine.* April 11, 2022. *greatergood. berkeley.edu/article/item/how_strong_is_your_sense_of_purpose_ in_life#:~:text=According%20to%20research%2C%20having%20 purpose,have%20better%20health%20and%20longevity.*

Stewart, Leilanie. "How Many People Who Write a Novel Finish It and How Many Get Published?" leilaniestewart.com. March 16, 2022. *leilaniestewart.com/2022/03/16/how-many-people-who-write-a-novel-finish-it-and-how-many-get-published/.*

Turayhi, Yasmeen. "How to Finally Finish Your Book." Medium. September 7, 2021. *yasmeenturayhi.medium.com/i-recently-learned-that-over-82-of-americans-want-to-write-a-book-but-less-than-1-of-americans-492cd5c900c8#:~:text=Socrates%20said%20%E2%80%9CThe%20 unexamined%20life,enough%E2%80%9D%2C%20and%20how%20 you%20react.*

University of Cambridge. "Reading for Pleasure Early in Childhood Linked to Better Cognitive Performance and Mental Wellbeing in Adolescence." EurekAlert! June 27, 2023. *www.eurekalert.org/news-releases/993270.*

White, Duncan. *Nabokov and His Books: Between Late Modernism and the Literary Marketplace.* Oxford University Press, 2017.

Made in United States
Troutdale, OR
01/23/2025

28260294R00149